STEPS
MATHEMATICS

Collins Educational
An imprint of HarperCollins*Publishers*

STEPS Answer Book 3b

ISBN 0 00 312576 9

Published 1994 by Collins Educational
An imprint of HarperCollins*Publishers*
77–85 Fulham Palace Road
London W6 8JB

Reprinted 1995

STEPS MATHEMATICS
Series Editor: **Anne Woodman**
Co-Editor: Paul Harling
Consultant Editor: Eric Albany

Design: Eric Drewery
Setting: TJ Graphics
Printed in Hong Kong

STEPS
MATHEMATICS

3b

Answer Book

INTRODUCTION

EVALUATING CHILDREN'S WORK

In line with the Non-Statutory Guidance (June 1989, para. 7.7), the activities in the STEPS Handbooks, Textbooks and Resource Masters provide both closed and 'open-ended' investigative tasks. The closed tasks help to ensure systematic coverage of the programmes of study; the open-ended tasks, in which different approaches and outcomes are possible, allow children to find their own level and explore without mathematical boundaries being imposed. Investigative tasks also offer the best opportunities for the teacher to assess attainment in relation to AT1.

Similarly, the overall 'feel' of the activities, open and closed, has been influenced by the programme of study for AT1, level 3 as recommended in paragraph 4 of the Non-Statutory Guidance (December 1991) which states that the SoAs (for AT1) *have ... been placed at levels where appropriate and challenging tasks can be set which are based on content defined at similar levels from the other ATs.*

GUIDANCE ON OPEN-ENDED TASKS WITHIN THE HANDBOOKS

Where open-ended tasks are suggested in the Activities in Detail in the Handbooks, and there is no supporting pupil material, guidance is generally given in the Handbook itself about what is likely to happen or to be observed .

TEXTBOOKS AND RESOURCE MASTERS

This book gives answers to closed tasks and guidance on assessing the open-ended tasks which appear in the pupils' materials (Textbooks and Resource Masters). This guidance takes the form of notes, some possible solutions, etc. but, in addition, you will see bracketed references to SoAs for Attainment Target 1 (Mathematics in the National Curriculum, December 1992). These references suggest the *baseline* SoA a child is most likely to show some evidence of achieving. Some children will achieve at levels beyond these and familiarity with the ATs, including AT1 and the strands will help you decide afterwards.

Please note: These bracketed references are only suggestions of the SoAs most likely to be demonstrated in the performance of the task. **1/3a** means Attainment Target **1**, level **3**, statement **a.** Abbreviated SoAs are usually written in the form Ma 1/3a where there is no supporting pupil material but, since all SoAs stated here are from Mathematics in the National Curriculum, the 'Ma' reference is omitted.

'MARKING' INVESTIGATIONAL WORK

Evaluating and commenting on investigational work is rather like commenting on a child's creative writing. It is 'personalised' work in which you can find out about the child as a creative mathematician and gain some insight into that child's understanding of mathematics, i.e. a powerful means of formative assessment. In investigatory work, not only is the mathematical content important, but also the process skills which children draw on to enable them to solve problems, some of which are included within AT1.

Conventional marking systems, traditionally ✔ or ✘, do not apply to investigational work, nor is it always necessary or, indeed, sustainable in terms of teacher time and effort to 'mark' everything written down. Very often you can get a intuitive feel – an overview – by focusing on parts of a child's recorded work. Apart from the mathematical content, you may be able to make some assessment in relation to AT1. This can be translated into a comment written on the work by you with the date, any SoA which you consider attained in view of this work, and comments by the child.

RECORD KEEPING

Whether you use the STEPS record-keeping sheets or your own school design, you might use a key for examples of closed or open-ended work selected as evidence of attaining a SoA e.g.
F for storage in a child's folder, **W** for an entry in a workbook,
O for observed evidence, etc.

Anne Woodman
Series Editor

TEXT BOOK PAGES

BOOK 3b
PAGE 1

Bar charts

RM 1

Work with a friend if you can.

Peter found the lengths of words on some pages of a book by counting letters.

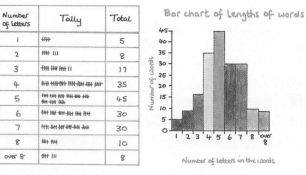

Tally Chart

Number of letters	Tally	Total
1	~~||||~~	5
2	~~||||~~ |||	8
3	~~||||~~ ~~||||~~ ~~||||~~ ||	17
4	~~||||~~ ~~||||~~ ~~||||~~ ~~||||~~ ~~||||~~ ~~||||~~ ~~||||~~	35
5	~~||||~~ ~~||||~~ ~~||||~~ ~~||||~~ ~~||||~~ ~~||||~~ ~~||||~~ ~~||||~~ ~~||||~~	45
6	~~||||~~ ~~||||~~ ~~||||~~ ~~||||~~ ~~||||~~ ~~||||~~	30
7	~~||||~~ ~~||||~~ ~~||||~~ ~~||||~~ ~~||||~~ ~~||||~~	30
8	~~||||~~ ~~||||~~	10
over 8	~~||||~~ |||	8

Bar chart of lengths of words

1 List the word lengths in order, most common first.

2 How many 5-letter words were there?

3 Choose a reading book. Make a tally chart **and** a bar chart of lengths of some words on a page. Use RM1 to help you draw the bar chart.

4 Write three ways in which your bar chart is different from Peter's.

STEPS 3b:1

1

5 letters,
4 letters,
6 letters/7 letters,
3 letters, 8 letters,
2 letters/over 8 letters,
1 letter.

45 5-letter words.

3

Practical: Making a tally chart and a bar chart of the lengths of some words on a page from a chosen reading book. (1/3 c)

Open: Listing 3 ways in which own and original graphs differ.

BOOK 3b PAGE 2

Pictograms

RM2

This **pictogram** shows the different newspapers taken by the families of Avril's friends.

Title	Newspapers taken by the families of my friends
key	stands for 4 families
Sun	
Daily Telegraph	
Daily Mail	
The Guardian	
Daily Mirror	
The Times	
The Independent	
Daily Express	

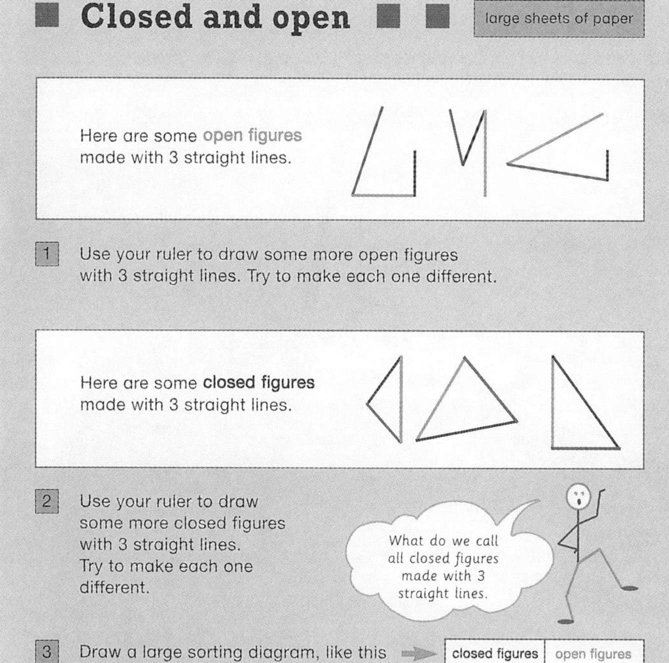

1 How many families do these symbols represent?

a

b

c

2 Use the pictogram to answer these.

a How many families take the *Daily Mirror*?
b How many families take the *Sun*?
c Which newspaper is taken by 5 families?
d Which newspaper is taken by 10 families?

3 List the newspapers in order with the one taken by most families first.

4 Survey your friends about newspapers taken by their families. Tally the data. Use RM2 to draw a pictogram of the results.

Work out how many newspapers are taken altogether in Avril's survey.

BOOK 3b PAGE 3

Closed and open

large sheets of paper

Here are some **open figures** made with 3 straight lines.

1 Use your ruler to draw some more open figures with 3 straight lines. Try to make each one different.

Here are some **closed figures** made with 3 straight lines.

2 Use your ruler to draw some more closed figures with 3 straight lines. Try to make each one different.

What do we call all closed figures made with 3 straight lines.

3 Draw a large sorting diagram, like this and label it.

Draw some figures in each region.

closed figures	open figures

1
a 1
b 2
c 3

2
a 13
b 12
c Daily Telegraph
d Daily Mail

3
Daily Mirror
Sun
Daily Mail
Daily Express
Daily Telegraph
The Guardian
The Independent
The Times

4
Open: Making a tally and pictogram of results from a survey of friends' newspapers. (1/3 b,c)

Challenge

57 altogether.

1
Practical: Drawing different open figures made from 3 straight lines.

2
Practical: Drawing different closed figures made from 3 straight lines (triangles).

3
Open: sorting open and closed figures. (1/3 b,c)

BOOK 3b
PAGE 4

All kinds of lines

1 Find examples of:
- vertical
- horizontal
- parallel
- diagonal lines.

Find patterns of lines and lines at right angles to each other.

4 STEPS 3b:2

Multiplication

1 Copy and complete.

a 5 × 2 = □		b 3 × □ = 12
c 6 × □ = 24		d 4 × □ = 16
e 1 × □ = 1		f 0 × 5 = □
g □ × 5 = 25		h 3 × 0 = □
i □ × 3 = 15		j 2 × □ = 14

2 Find at least four different answers to each of these.

a 5 × □ = □ b □ × 3 = □ c 4 × □ = □

3 Write < or > between each pair of multiplications.

a 6 × 2 3 × 5
b 2 × 1 5 × 0
c 3 × 3 4 × 2
d 3 × 4 5 × 2
e 5 × 3 4 × 4

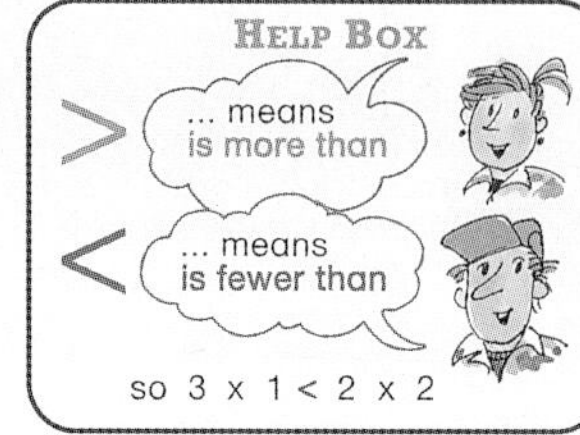
HELP BOX
> ... means is more than
< ... means is fewer than
so 3 x 1 < 2 x 2

CHALLENGE

Use these numbers and signs as often as you like to make different sentences.
For example 16 ÷ 8 = 2

0 1 2 4 8 16
× ÷ =

STEPS 3b:3 5

BOOK 3b
PAGE 5

1

Identifying examples of vertical, horizontal, parallel and diagonal lines. Finding patterns of lines at right angles to each other. (1/3 c, 1/4 b)

2

Open: Finding at least four different answers for each part. For example:

a	b	c
5 x 2 = 10	1 x 3 = 3	4 x 8 = 32
5 x 4 = 20	3 x 3 = 9	4 x 6 = 24
5 x 3 = 15	0 x 3 = 0	4 x 2 = 8
5 x 7 = 35	9 x 3 = 27	4 x 3 = 12
		(1/3 a,b)

3

a 6 x 2 < 3 x 5 **b** 2 x 1 > 5 x 0 **c** 3 x 3 > 4 x 2

d 3 x 4 > 5 x 2 **e** 5 x 3 < 4 x 4 (1/3 a,b)

1

a 5 x 2 = 10

b 3 x 4 = 12

c 6 x 4 = 24

d 4 x 4 = 16

e 1 x 1 = 1

f 0 x 5 = 0

g 5 x 5 = 25

h 3 x 0 = 0

i 5 x 3 = 15

j 2 x 7 = 14

Challenge

Using 0, 1, 2, 4, 8, 16 and signs x , ÷, = to make different sentences.
(1/3 a,b)

BOOK 3b PAGE 6

Team tables

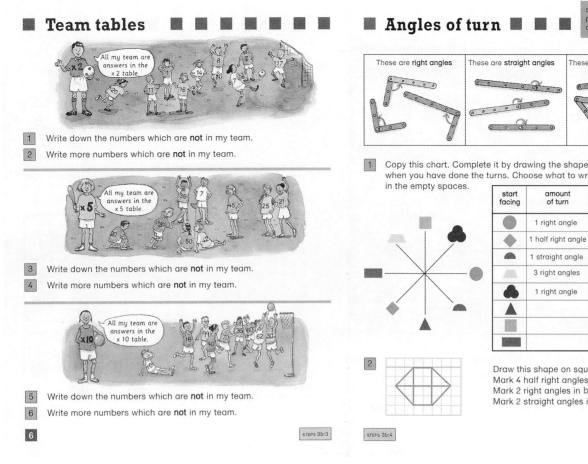

1 Write down the numbers which are **not** in my team.

2 Write more numbers which are **not** in my team.

3 Write down the numbers which are **not** in my team.

4 Write more numbers which are **not** in my team.

5 Write down the numbers which are **not** in my team.

6 Write more numbers which are **not** in my team.

BOOK 3b PAGE 7

Angles of turn

squared paper, paper half right angle

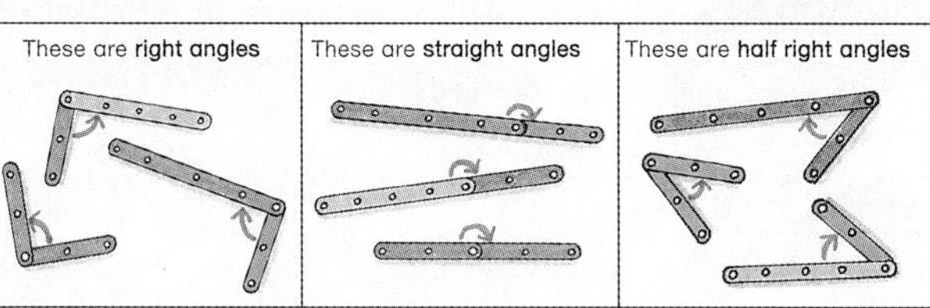

1 Copy this chart. Complete it by drawing the shape you will face when you have done the turns. Choose what to write or draw in the empty spaces.

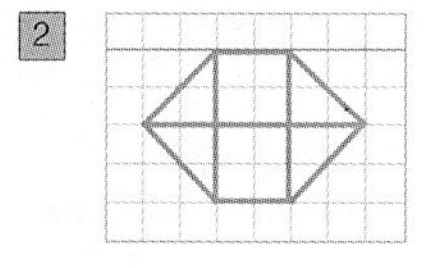

start facing	amount of turn	direction of turn	end facing
circle	1 right angle	clockwise	triangle
diamond	1 half right angle	anticlockwise	
semicircle	1 straight angle	clockwise	
trapezium	3 right angles	anticlockwise	
club	1 right angle		
triangle		anticlockwise	
square			
rectangle			

2 Draw this shape on squared paper.
Mark 4 half right angles in green.
Mark 2 right angles in blue.
Mark 2 straight angles in red.

1

11, 1, 7, 17

2

3, 5, 9, 13, ...(any odd numbers).

3

36, 7, 42, 21

4

1, 2, 3, 4, 6, 8, 9, ...(numbers which are **not** multiples of 5).

5

16, 99, 35, 62

6

1, 2, 3, 21, 37, 84, ...(numbers which are **not** multiples of 10).

1

start facing	amount of turn	direction of turn	end facing
circle	1 right angle	clockwise	triangle
diamond	1 half right angle	anticlockwise	trapezium
semicircle	1 straight angle	clockwise	trapezium
trapezium	3 right angles	anticlockwise	club
club	1 right angle		
triangle		anticlockwise	
square			
rectangle			

2

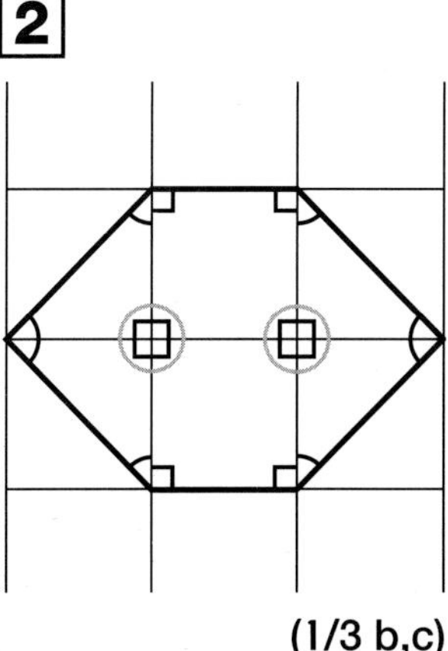

(1/3 b,c)

BOOK 3b
PAGE 8

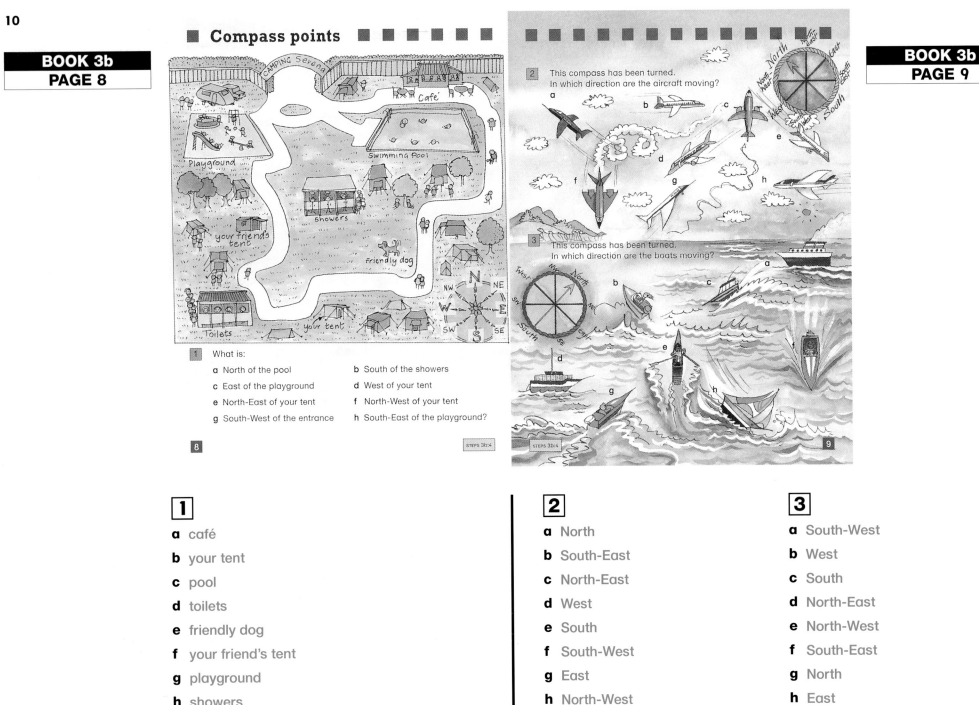

Compass points

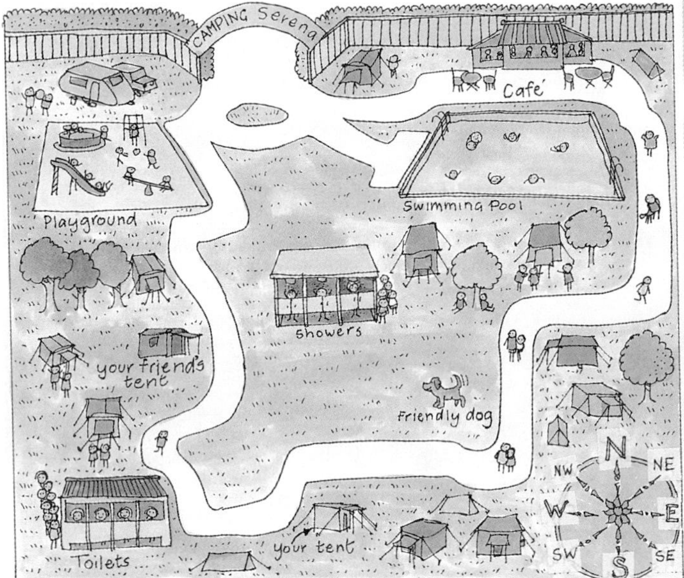

1 What is:

a North of the pool
b South of the showers
c East of the playground
d West of your tent
e North-East of your tent
f North-West of your tent
g South-West of the entrance
h South-East of the playground?

8 STEPS 3b:4

BOOK 3b
PAGE 9

2 This compass has been turned.
In which direction are the aircraft moving?

3 This compass has been turned.
In which direction are the boats moving?

STEPS 3b:4 9

a café
b your tent
c pool
d toilets
e friendly dog
f your friend's tent
g playground
h showers

2

a North
b South-East
c North-East
d West
e South
f South-West
g East
h North-West

3

a South-West
b West
c South
d North-East
e North-West
f South-East
g North
h East

BOOK 3b PAGE 10

a.m. and p.m.

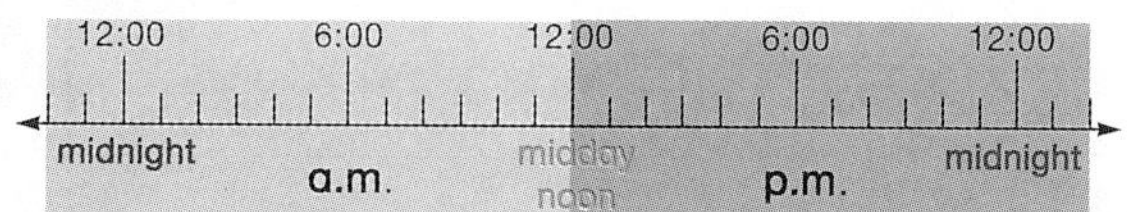

1 Are these times before or after midday?

a 7 a.m. b 11 p.m. c 6 p.m. d 10 a.m.

Use the time line to help you with questions 1,2 and 3.

2 Are these times before or after **midnight**?

a 3 a.m. b 11 a.m. c 8 p.m. d 10 a.m.

3 Write these times in order, earliest first.

11 a.m. | 3 p.m. | 9 p.m. | 4 a.m. | noon

4 Write each of these in numbers. Label it a.m. or p.m.

a one hour before midnight b one hour after midday

5 Do you normally do these things a.m. or p.m. or both?

a eat breakfast b watch television c sleep
d travel to school e start school f finish school

6 How many hours between these times?

a 9 a.m. and 3 p.m. b 6 a.m. and 6 p.m.
c 10 p.m. and 6 a.m. d 6 a.m. and 11 a.m.
e midnight and midday f midday and the next midday

10 STEPS 3b:5

BOOK 3b PAGE 11

Analogue times

analogue clock face

1 Write each time in words.

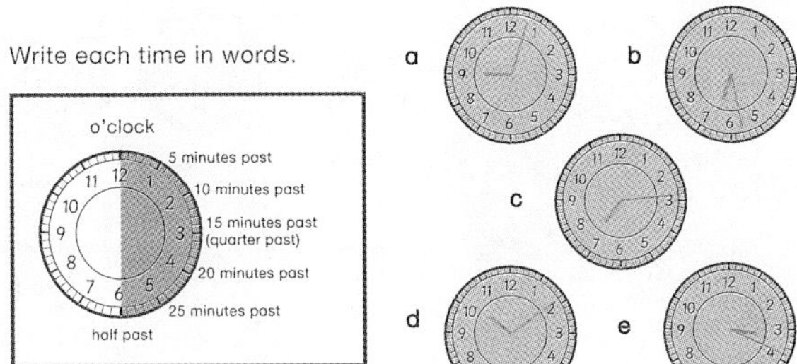

a b c d e

2 Write each time in words.

o'clock
5 minutes to
10 minutes to
15 minutes to (quarter to)
20 minutes to
25 minutes to

a b c d e

3 This clock shows it is now 8.21. What time was it:

a 2 hours ago
b 15 minutes ago
c half an hour ago?

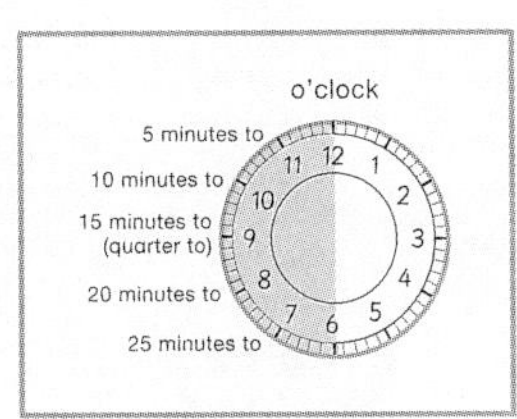

4 What time will it be on the same clock in:

a 2 hours b 25 minutes c half an hour?

STEPS 3b:5 11

Page 10 answers

1
a before
b after
c after
d before

2
a after
b after
c before
d after

3
4 a.m.
11 a.m.
noon
3 p.m.
9 p.m.

4
a 11 p.m.
b 1 p.m.

5
a a.m.
b p.m.
c p.m.
d a.m.
e a.m.
f p.m.

6
a 6 hours b 12 hours c 8 hours
d 5 hours e 12 hours f 24 hours

Page 11 answers

1
a 3 minutes past 9 b 28 minutes past 6 c 14 minutes past 7
d 9 minutes past 10 e 19 minutes past 3

2
a 17 minutes to 11
b 2 minutes to 8
c 21 minutes to 7
d 24 minutes to 3
e 9 minutes to 12

3
a 21 minutes past 6 (6.21)
b 6 minutes past 8 (8.06)
c 9 minutes to 8 (7.51)

4
a 21 minutes past 10 (10.21)
b 14 minutes to 9 (8.46)
c 9 minutes to 9 (8.51)

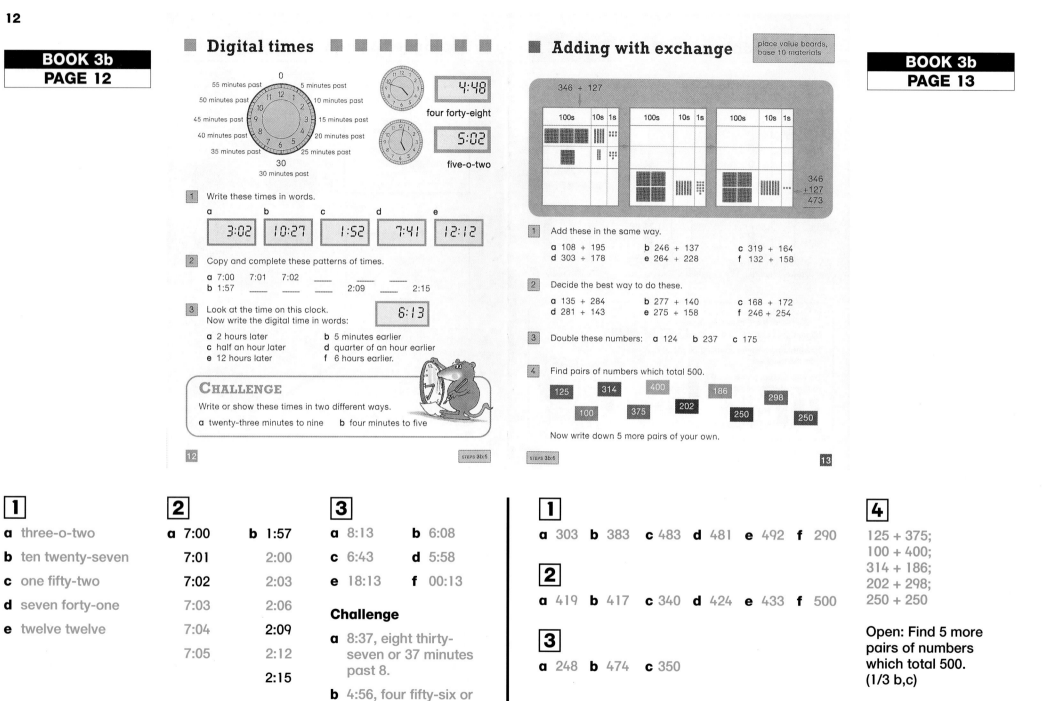

BOOK 3b PAGE 12

Digital times

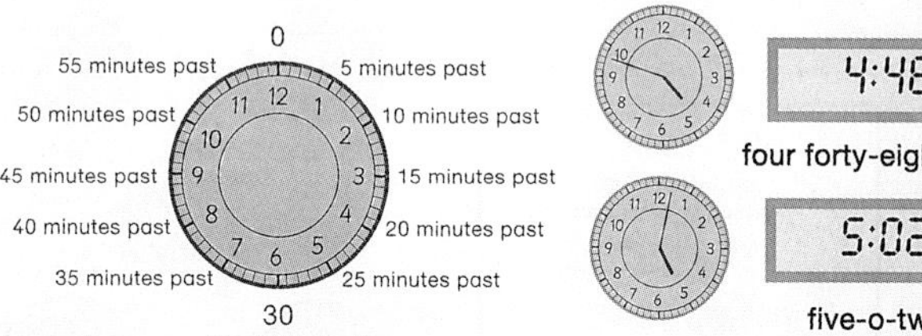

4:48
four forty-eight

5:02
five-o-two

1 Write these times in words.

a 3:02 b 10:27 c 1:52 d 7:41 e 12:12

2 Copy and complete these patterns of times.

a 7:00 7:01 7:02 ___ ___ ___
b 1:57 ___ ___ ___ 2:09 ___ 2:15

3 Look at the time on this clock. 6:13
Now write the digital time in words:

a 2 hours later
b 5 minutes earlier
c half an hour later
d quarter of an hour earlier
e 12 hours later
f 6 hours earlier.

CHALLENGE

Write or show these times in two different ways.

a twenty-three minutes to nine
b four minutes to five

Adding with exchange

place value boards, base 10 materials

BOOK 3b PAGE 13

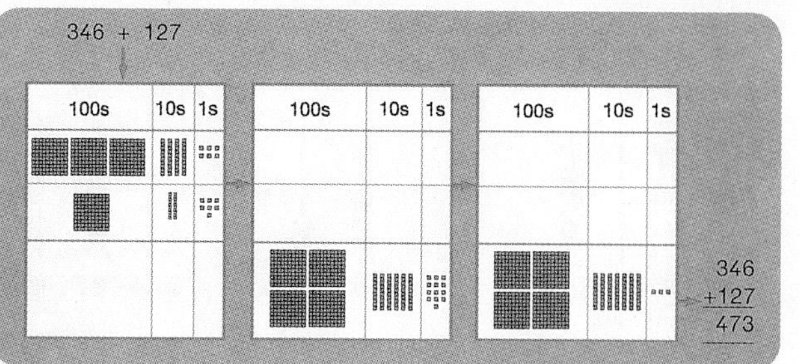

1 Add these in the same way.

a 108 + 195 b 246 + 137 c 319 + 164
d 303 + 178 e 264 + 228 f 132 + 158

2 Decide the best way to do these.

a 135 + 284 b 277 + 140 c 168 + 172
d 281 + 143 e 275 + 158 f 246 + 254

3 Double these numbers: a 124 b 237 c 175

4 Find pairs of numbers which total 500.

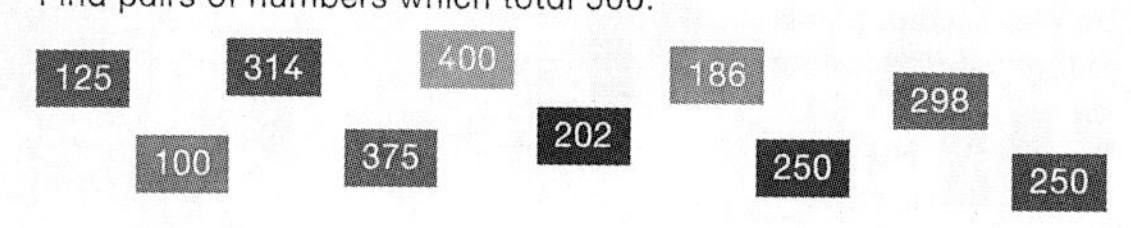

Now write down 5 more pairs of your own.

1

a three-o-two
b ten twenty-seven
c one fifty-two
d seven forty-one
e twelve twelve

2

a	b
7:00	1:57
7:01	2:00
7:02	2:03
7:03	2:06
7:04	2:09
7:05	2:12
	2:15

3

a 8:13 b 6:08
c 6:43 d 5:58
e 18:13 f 00:13

Challenge

a 8:37, eight thirty-seven or 37 minutes past 8.

b 4:56, four fifty-six or 56 minutes past 6.

1

a 303 b 383 c 483 d 481 e 492 f 290

2

a 419 b 417 c 340 d 424 e 433 f 500

3

a 248 b 474 c 350

4

125 + 375;
100 + 400;
314 + 186;
202 + 298;
250 + 250

Open: Find 5 more pairs of numbers which total 500. (1/3 b,c)

BOOK 3b
PAGE 14

More adding

abacus and beads, 5 small blank cards

1 Add 143 to each of these.
Write down each sum in your own way.

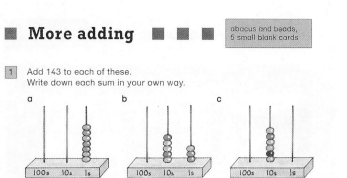

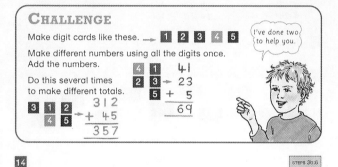

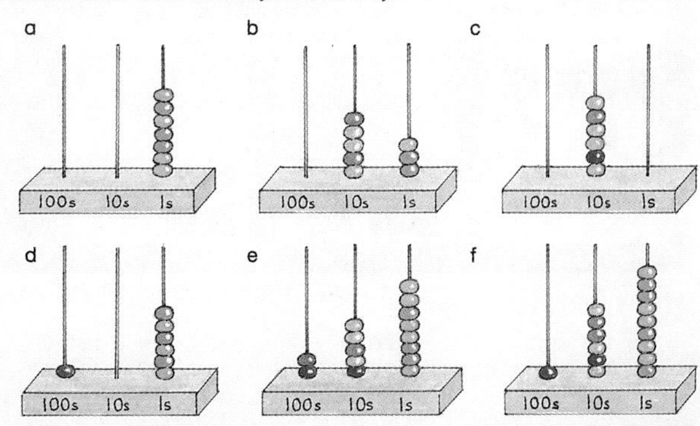

CHALLENGE

Make digit cards like these. → 1 2 3 4 5

Make different numbers using all the digits once.
Add the numbers.

Do this several times to make different totals.

3 1 2 → 312 + 45 = 357
4 5

4 1 → 41
2 3 → 23
5 → + 5 = 69

BOOK 3b
PAGE 15

Addition problems

Solve these problems in any way you like.
Write down how you worked out the answers.

1 Miss Adams works at the Post Office. On her busiest day she sold 227 first class stamps and 185 second class stamps. How many stamps did she sell altogether?

2 Ms Simms, the car park attendant, sold 123 parking tickets on Monday. On Tuesday she sold 10 more tickets than on Monday. How many tickets did she sell altogether on the two days?

3 Mr Bell, in the fruit shop, bought two boxes of oranges, each with the same number inside.
Altogether, there were 186. How many in each box?

CHALLENGE

On Tuesday and Wednesday, Mr and Mrs Lee sold 96 comics altogether. They sold ten more on Tuesday than on Wednesday.
How many comics did they sell:
a on Tuesday? b on Wednesday?

1

a 150
b 196
c 203
d 149
e 401
f 312

Challenge

Add numbers made from the digits 1, 2, 3, 4 and 5 (many possibilities). (1/3 b)

1

412 stamps

2

256 tickets

3

93 in each box

Challenge

a 53 on Tuesday
b 43 on Wednesday (1/3 a)

BOOK 3b
PAGE 16

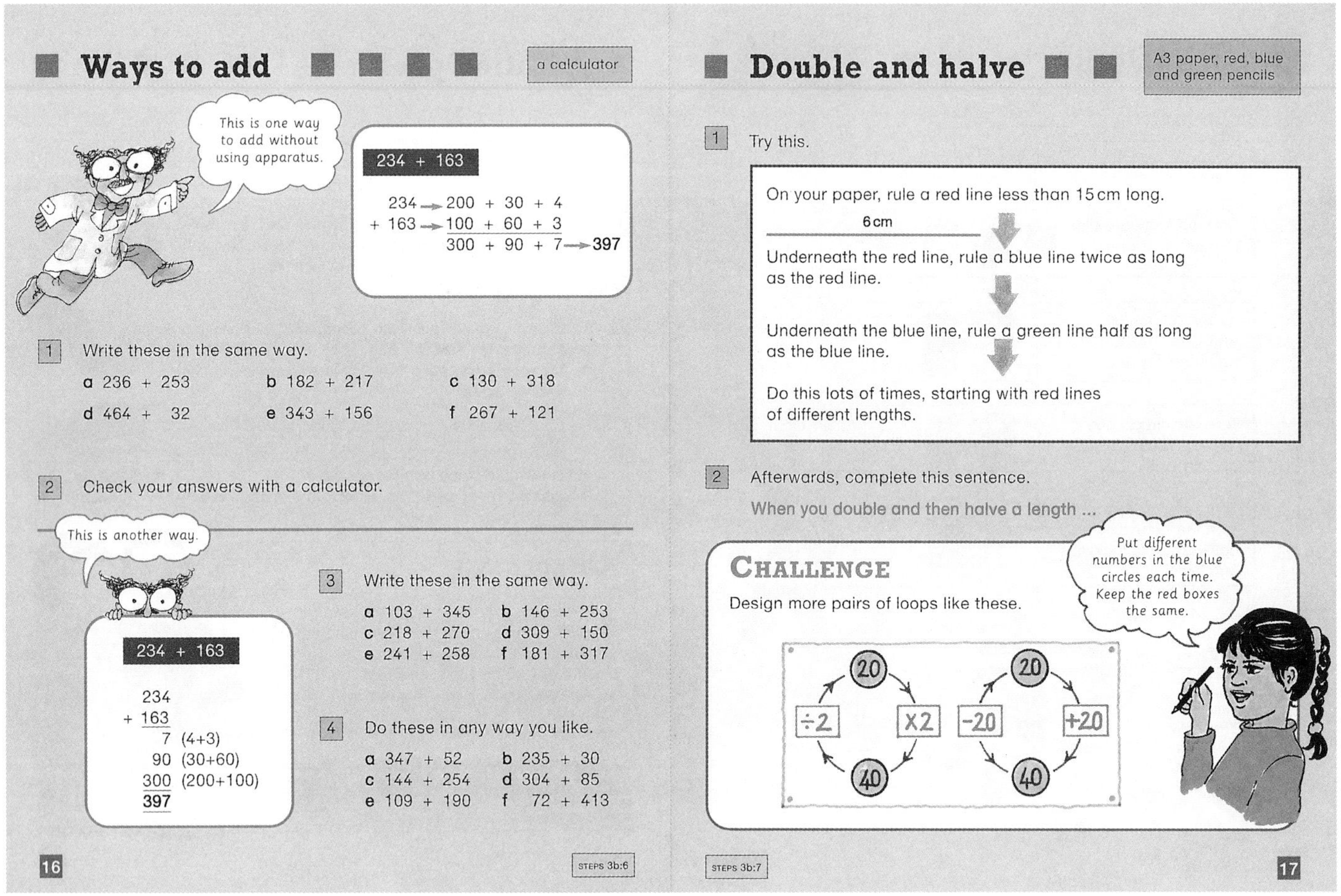

Ways to add

a calculator

This is one way to add without using apparatus.

234 + 163

```
  234 → 200 + 30 + 4
+ 163 → 100 + 60 + 3
        300 + 90 + 7 → 397
```

1 Write these in the same way.

a 236 + 253 b 182 + 217 c 130 + 318

d 464 + 32 e 343 + 156 f 267 + 121

2 Check your answers with a calculator.

This is another way.

234 + 163

```
  234
+ 163
    7  (4+3)
   90  (30+60)
  300  (200+100)
  397
```

3 Write these in the same way.

a 103 + 345 b 146 + 253

c 218 + 270 d 309 + 150

e 241 + 258 f 181 + 317

4 Do these in any way you like.

a 347 + 52 b 235 + 30

c 144 + 254 d 304 + 85

e 109 + 190 f 72 + 413

Double and halve

A3 paper, red, blue and green pencils

1 Try this.

On your paper, rule a red line less than 15 cm long.

6 cm

Underneath the red line, rule a blue line twice as long as the red line.

Underneath the blue line, rule a green line half as long as the blue line.

Do this lots of times, starting with red lines of different lengths.

2 Afterwards, complete this sentence.

When you double and then halve a length ...

CHALLENGE

Design more pairs of loops like these.

Put different numbers in the blue circles each time. Keep the red boxes the same.
20
÷2
X2
40
20
-20
+20
40

BOOK 3b
PAGE 17

1

Pratical: ruling lines.

2

When you double and then halve a length you have the length you started with.

Challenge

Designing loops to show halving and doubling. (1/3 b,c,d)

1

```
a   236 → 200 + 30 + 6
  + 253 → 200 + 50 + 3
          400 + 80 + 9 → 489

b   182 → 100 + 80 + 2
  + 217 → 200 + 10 + 7
          300 + 90 + 9 → 399

c   130 → 100 + 30 + 0
  + 318 → 300 + 10 + 8
          400 + 40 + 8 → 448

d   464 → 400 + 60 + 4
  +  32 →       30 + 2
          400 + 90 + 6 → 496

e   343 → 300 + 40 + 3
  + 156 → 100 + 50 + 6
          400 + 90 + 9 → 499

f   267 → 200 + 60 + 7
  + 121 → 100 + 20 + 1
          300 + 80 + 8 → 388
```

2

Check answers on calculator.

3

```
a   103
  + 345
      8  (3+5)
     40  (0+40)
    400  (100+300)
    448

b   146
  + 253
      9  (6+3)
     90  (40+50)
    300  (100+200)
    399

c   218
  + 270
      8  (8+0)
     80  (10+70)
    400  (200+200)
    488

d   309
  + 150
      9  (9+0)
     50  (0+50)
    400  (300+100)
    499

e   241
  + 258
      9  (1+8)
     90  (40+50)
    400  (200+200)
    499

f   181
  + 317
      8  (1+7)
     90  (80+10)
    400  (100+300)
    498
```

4

a 399 b 265 c 398

d 389 e 299 f 485

BOOK 3b
PAGE 18

Back to the start!

Polydron or Clixi tiles, colouring materials to match

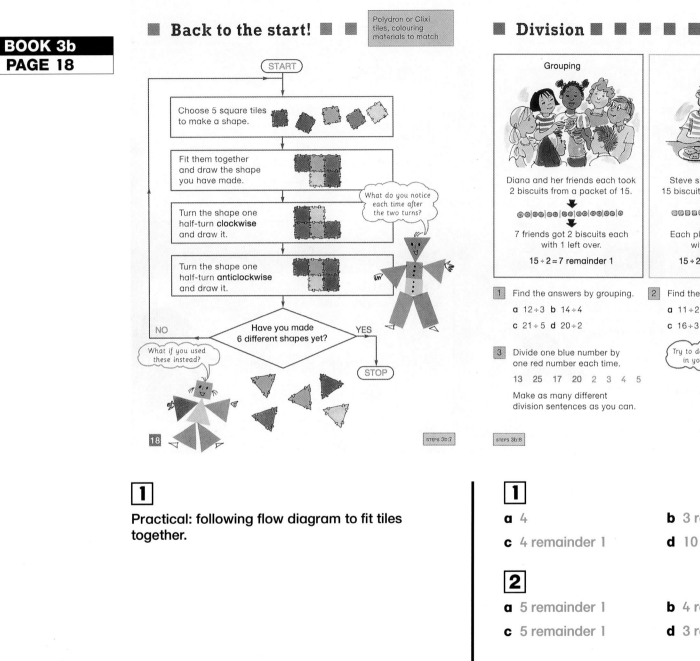

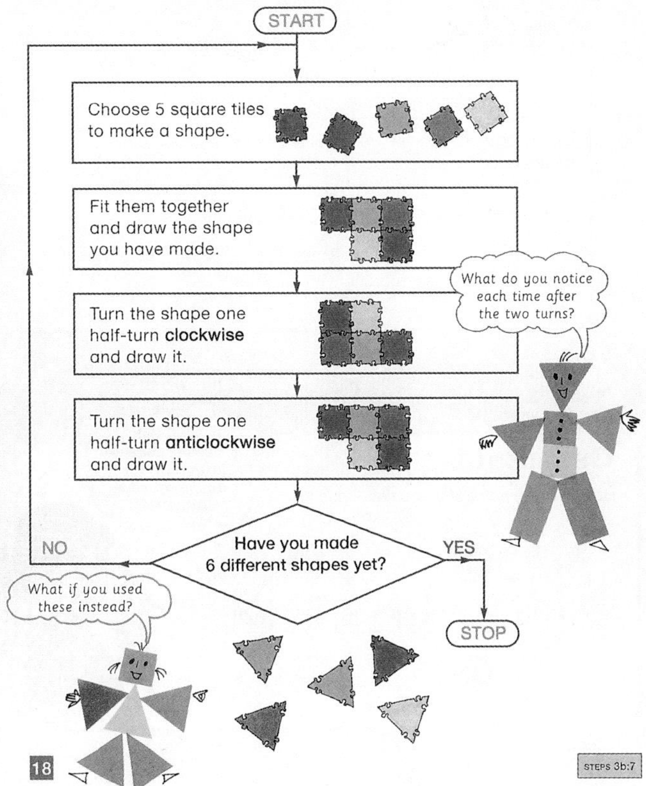

START
Choose 5 square tiles to make a shape.
Fit them together and draw the shape you have made.
Turn the shape one half-turn clockwise and draw it.
Turn the shape one half-turn anticlockwise and draw it.
What do you notice each time after the two turns?
Have you made 6 different shapes yet?
NO
YES
STOP
What if you used these instead?

18 STEPS 3b:7

BOOK 3b
PAGE 19

Division

counting objects

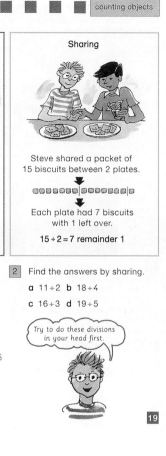

Grouping

Diana and her friends each took 2 biscuits from a packet of 15.

7 friends got 2 biscuits each with 1 left over.

15 ÷ 2 = 7 remainder 1

Sharing

Steve shared a packet of 15 biscuits between 2 plates.

Each plate had 7 biscuits with 1 left over.

15 ÷ 2 = 7 remainder 1

1 Find the answers by grouping.

a 12 ÷ 3 b 14 ÷ 4

c 21 ÷ 5 d 20 ÷ 2

2 Find the answers by sharing.

a 11 ÷ 2 b 18 ÷ 4

c 16 ÷ 3 d 19 ÷ 5

3 Divide one blue number by one red number each time.

13 25 17 20 2 3 4 5

Make as many different division sentences as you can.

Try to do these divisions in your head first.

STEPS 3b:8 19

1

Practical: following flow diagram to fit tiles together.

1

a 4 **b** 3 remainder 2

c 4 remainder 1 **d** 10

2

a 5 remainder 1 **b** 4 remainder 2

c 5 remainder 1 **d** 3 remainder 4

3

13 ÷ 2 = 6 remainder 1
13 ÷ 3 = 4 remainder 1
13 ÷ 4 = 3 remainder 1
13 ÷ 5 = 2 remainder 3

25 ÷ 2 = 12 remainder 1
25 ÷ 3 = 8 remainder 1
25 ÷ 4 = 6 remainder 1
25 ÷ 5 = 5

17 ÷ 2 = 8 remainder 1
17 ÷ 3 = 5 remainder 2
17 ÷ 4 = 4 remainder 1
17 ÷ 5 = 3 remainder 2

20 ÷ 2 = 10
20 ÷ 3 = 6 remainder 2
20 ÷ 4 = 5
20 ÷ 5 = 4

BOOK 3b
PAGE 20

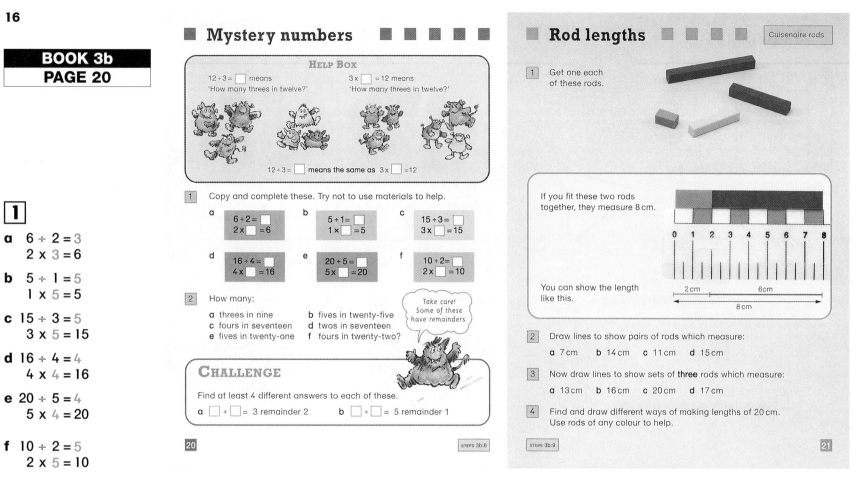

Mystery numbers

HELP BOX
12 ÷ 3 = ☐ means
'How many threes in twelve?'
3 x ☐ = 12 means
'How many threes in twelve?'
12 ÷ 3 = ☐ means the same as 3 x ☐ = 12

1 Copy and complete these. Try not to use materials to help.

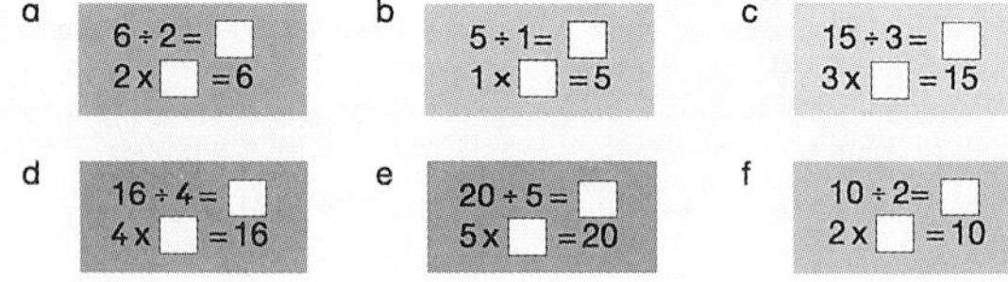

a	b	c
6 ÷ 2 = ☐ 2 x ☐ = 6	5 ÷ 1 = ☐ 1 x ☐ = 5	15 ÷ 3 = ☐ 3 x ☐ = 15
d	**e**	**f**
16 ÷ 4 = ☐ 4 x ☐ = 16	20 ÷ 5 = ☐ 5 x ☐ = 20	10 ÷ 2 = ☐ 2 x ☐ = 10

2 How many:

a threes in nine
b fives in twenty-five
c fours in seventeen
d twos in seventeen
e fives in twenty-one
f fours in twenty-two?

Take care! Some of these have remainders.

CHALLENGE

Find at least 4 different answers to each of these.

a ☐ ÷ ☐ = 3 remainder 2
b ☐ ÷ ☐ = 5 remainder 1

a 6 ÷ 2 = 3
2 x 3 = 6

b 5 ÷ 1 = 5
1 x 5 = 5

c 15 ÷ 3 = 5
3 x 5 = 15

d 16 ÷ 4 = 4
4 x 4 = 16

e 20 ÷ 5 = 4
5 x 4 = 20

f 10 ÷ 2 = 5
2 x 5 = 10

2

a three
b five
c four remainder one
d eight remainder one
e four remainder one
f five remainder two

Challenge

At least 4 examples similar to:

a 8 ÷ 2 = 3 remainder 2
11 ÷ 3 = 3 remainder 2

b 11 ÷ 2 = 5 remainder 1
16 ÷ 3 = 5 remainder 1
17 ÷ 5 = 3 remainder 2
31 ÷ 6 = 5 remainder 1
23 ÷ 7 = 3 remainder 2
46 ÷ 9 = 5 remainder 1 etc. (1/3 a,b)

BOOK 3b
PAGE 21

Rod lengths

Cuisenaire rods

1 Get one each of these rods.

If you fit these two rods together, they measure 8 cm.

0 1 2 3 4 5 6 7 8

You can show the length like this.

2 cm 6 cm
8 cm

2 Draw lines to show pairs of rods which measure:
a 7 cm b 14 cm c 11 cm d 15 cm

3 Now draw lines to show sets of **three** rods which measure:
a 13 cm b 16 cm c 20 cm d 17 cm

4 Find and draw different ways of making lengths of 20 cm. Use rods of any colour to help.

Practical: fitting rods together to make a given length.

Practical: drawing lines to show sets of three rods which measure:

a 13cm **b** 16cm
c 20cm **d** 17cm

Practical: drawing lines to show pairs of rods which measure:

a 7cm **b** 14cm
c 11cm **d** 15cm

Open: drawing different ways of making up a length of 20 cm.

BOOK 3b
PAGE 22

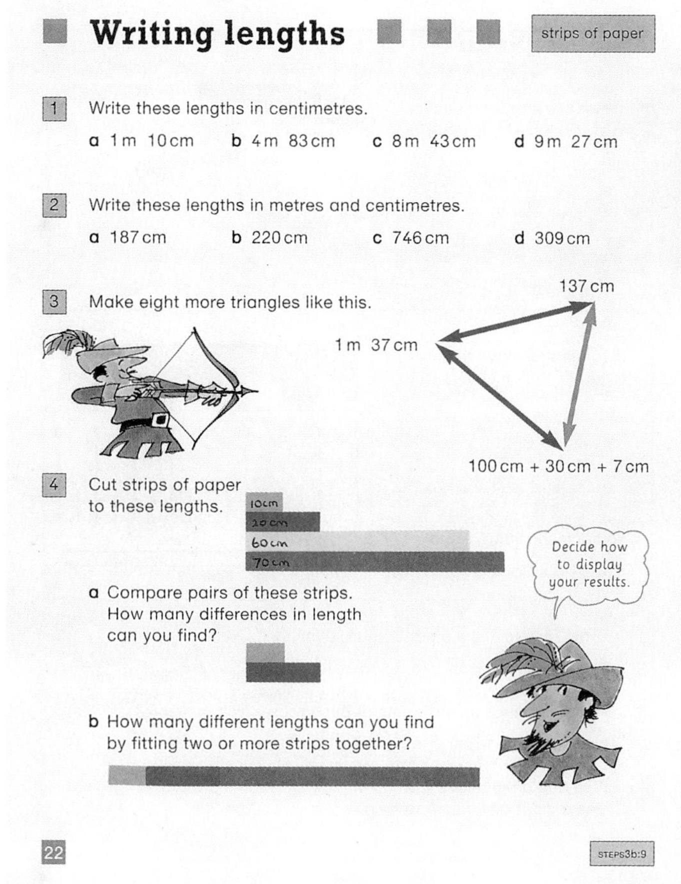

Writing lengths

strips of paper

1 Write these lengths in centimetres.

a 1 m 10 cm b 4 m 83 cm c 8 m 43 cm d 9 m 27 cm

2 Write these lengths in metres and centimetres.

a 187 cm b 220 cm c 746 cm d 309 cm

3 Make eight more triangles like this.

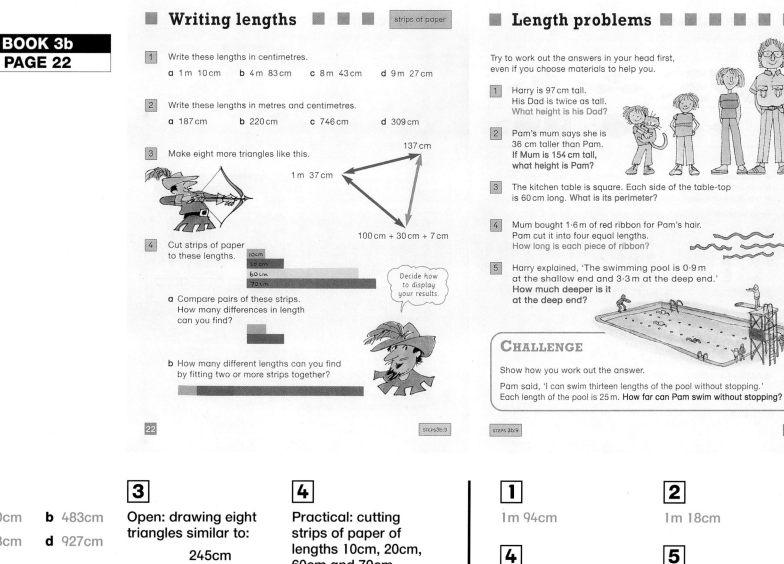

4 Cut strips of paper to these lengths.

a Compare pairs of these strips. How many differences in length can you find?

b How many different lengths can you find by fitting two or more strips together?

22 STEPS3b:9

BOOK 3b
PAGE 23

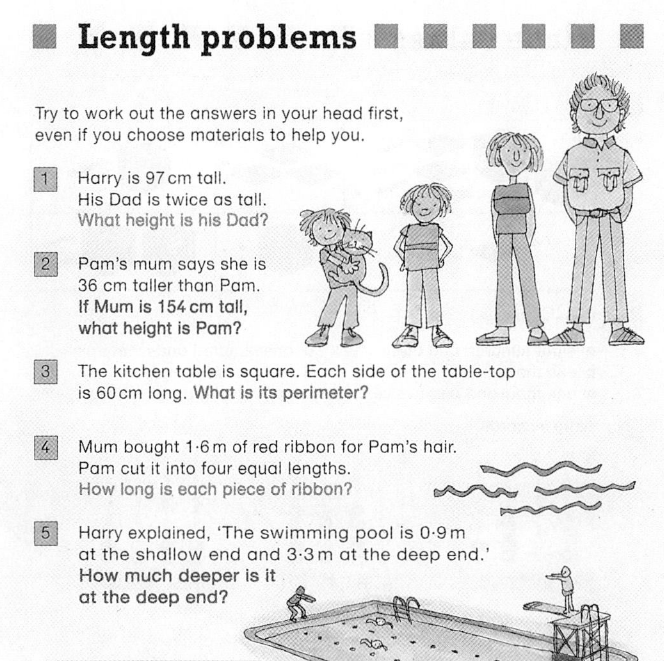

Length problems

Try to work out the answers in your head first, even if you choose materials to help you.

1 Harry is 97 cm tall. His Dad is twice as tall. What height is his Dad?

2 Pam's mum says she is 36 cm taller than Pam. If Mum is 154 cm tall, what height is Pam?

3 The kitchen table is square. Each side of the table-top is 60 cm long. What is its perimeter?

4 Mum bought 1·6 m of red ribbon for Pam's hair. Pam cut it into four equal lengths. How long is each piece of ribbon?

5 Harry explained, 'The swimming pool is 0·9 m at the shallow end and 3·3 m at the deep end.' How much deeper is it at the deep end?

CHALLENGE

Show how you work out the answer.

Pam said, 'I can swim thirteen lengths of the pool without stopping.' Each length of the pool is 25 m. How far can Pam swim without stopping?

STEPS 3b:9 23

1

a 110cm **b** 483cm

c 843cm **d** 927cm

2

a 1m 87cm

b 2m 20cm

c 7m 46cm

d 3m 9cm

3

Open: drawing eight triangles similar to:

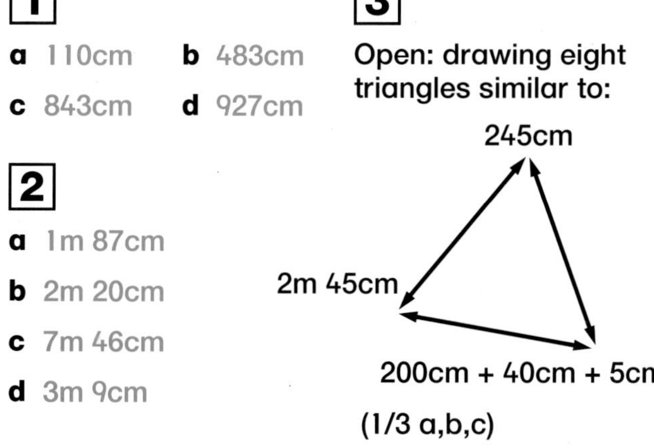

(1/3 a,b,c)

4

Practical: cutting strips of paper of lengths 10cm, 20cm, 60cm and 70cm

a Comparing pairs of strips to find differences in length.

b Fitting two or more strips together to make different lengths.
(1/3 a,b)

1

1m 94cm

2

1m 18cm

3

2m 40cm

4

40cm

5

2.4m or 2m 40cm

Challenge

25m x 13 = 325m
(1/3 a)

BOOK 3b PAGE 24

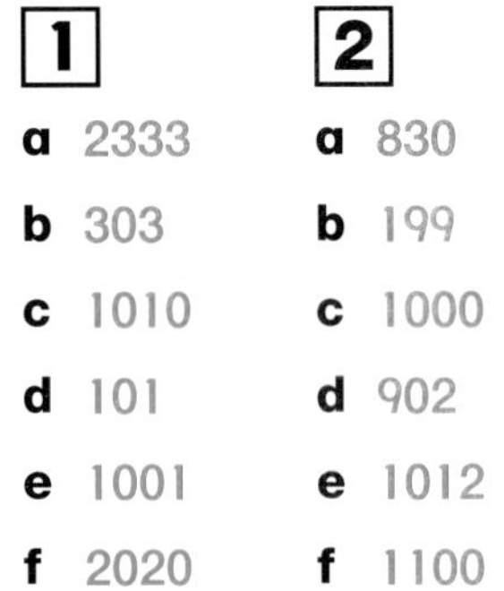

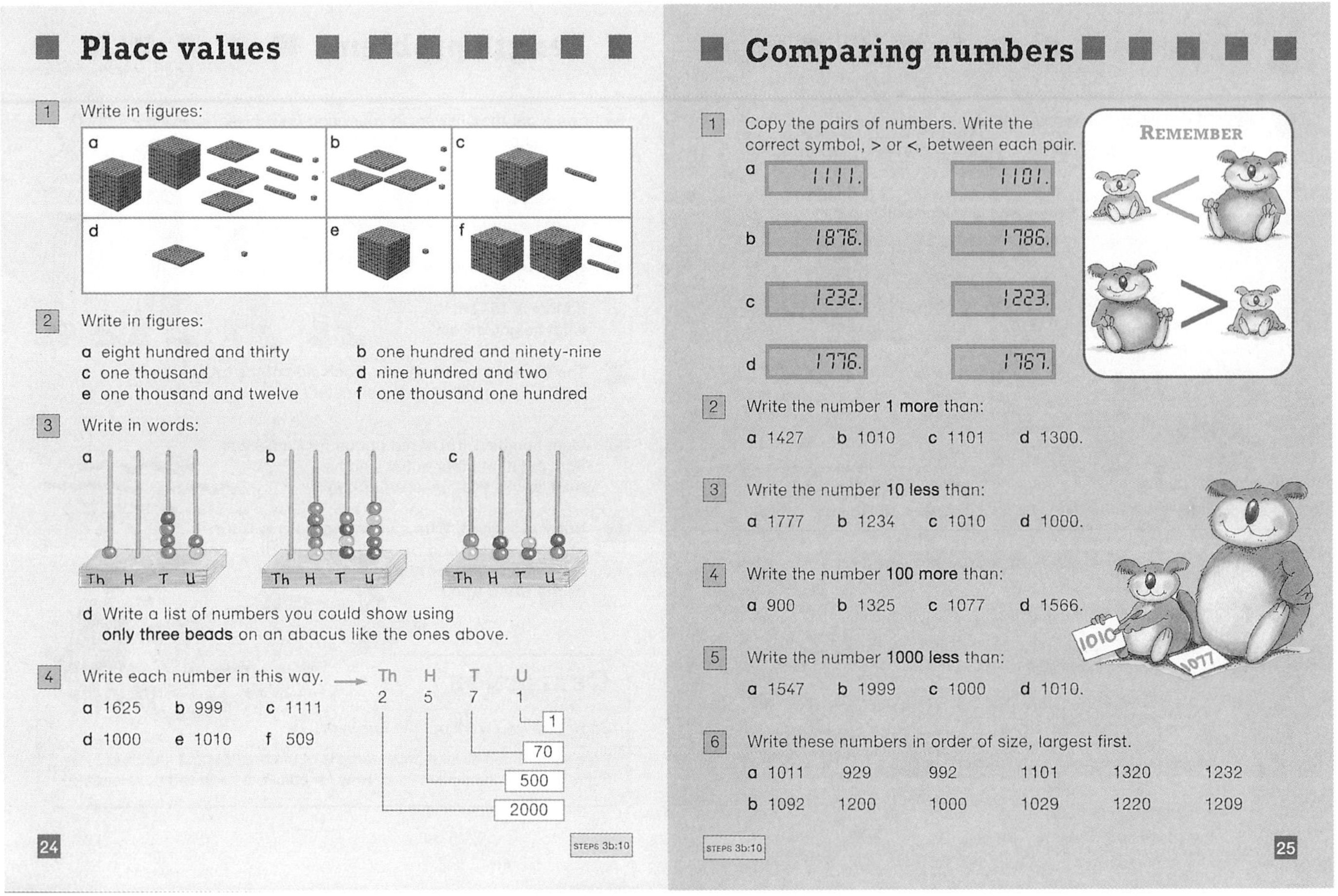

1

- **a** 2333
- **b** 303
- **c** 1010
- **d** 101
- **e** 1001
- **f** 2020

2

- **a** 830
- **b** 199
- **c** 1000
- **d** 902
- **e** 1012
- **f** 1100

3

- **a** one thousand and forty-two
- **b** five hundred and forty-five
- **c** two thousand two hundred and twenty-two
- **d** Open: a list of numbers showing only three beads on the 4-spike abacus. Many examples such as: 3000, 300, 30, 3, 2100, 2010, 2001, 1200, 1020, 1002, 1110, 1101, 1011, in which the digits add to 3. (1/3 a,c)

4

a

Th	H	T	U
1	6	2	5

5, 20, 600, 1000

b

Th	H	T	U
	9	9	9

9, 90, 900

c

Th	H	T	U
1	1	1	1

1, 10, 100, 1000

d 1 0 0 0 — 1000

e 1 0 1 0 — 10, 1000

f 5 0 9 — 9, 500

BOOK 3b PAGE 25

1

- **a** 1111 > 1101
- **b** 1876 > 1786
- **c** 1232 > 1223
- **d** 1776 > 1767

2

- **a** 1428 **b** 1011
- **c** 1102 **d** 1301

3

- **a** 1767 **b** 1224
- **c** 1000 **d** 990

4

- **a** 1000 **b** 1425
- **c** 1177 **d** 1666

5

- **a** 547 **b** 999
- **c** 0 **d** 10

6

a	b
1320	1220
1232	1209
1101	1200
1011	1092
992	1029
929	1000

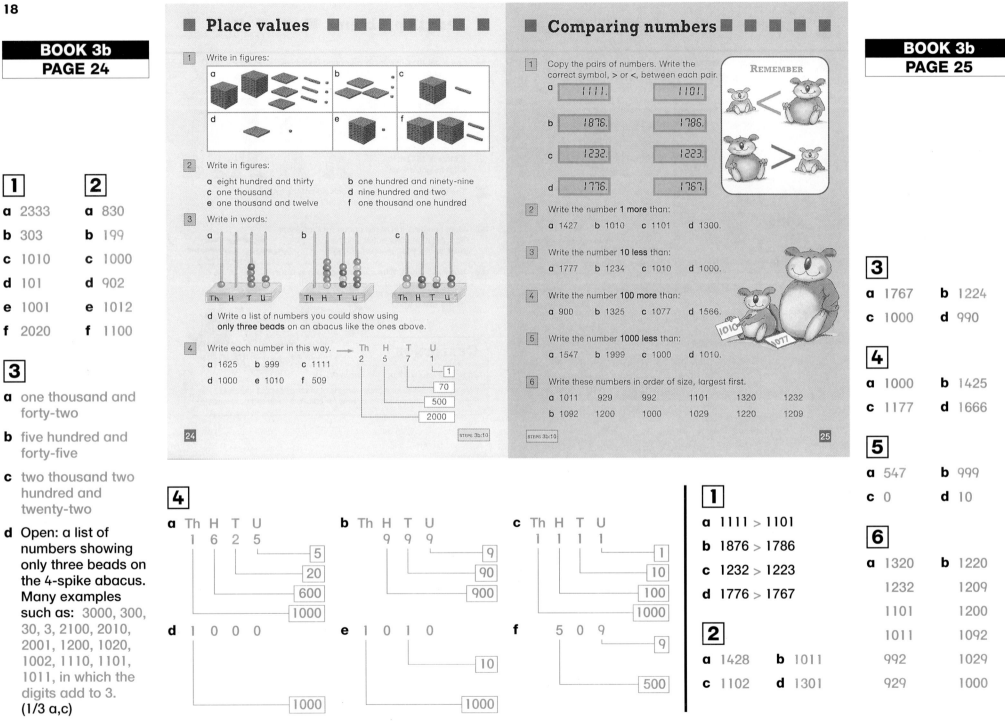

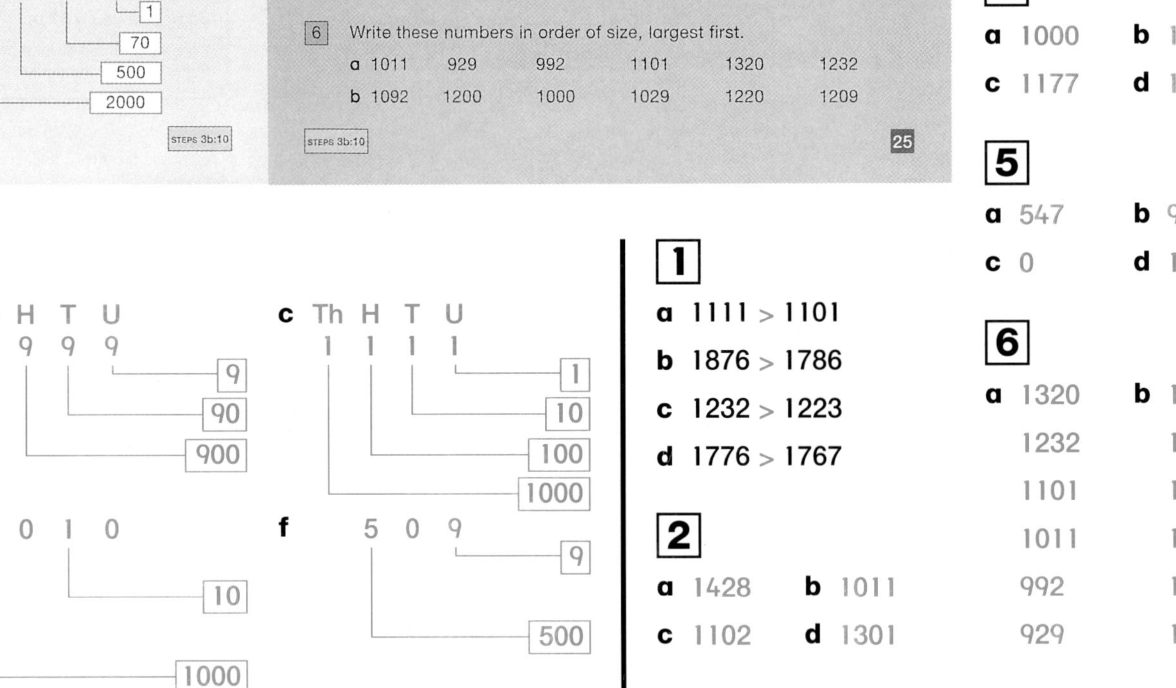

Place values

1 Write in figures:

a b c d e f

2 Write in figures:

- a eight hundred and thirty
- b one hundred and ninety-nine
- c one thousand
- d nine hundred and two
- e one thousand and twelve
- f one thousand one hundred

3 Write in words:

a Th H T U b Th H T U c Th H T U

d Write a list of numbers you could show using **only three beads** on an abacus like the ones above.

4 Write each number in this way. → Th H T U: 2 5 7 1 → 1, 70, 500, 2000

- a 1625
- b 999
- c 1111
- d 1000
- e 1010
- f 509

24 STEPS 3b:10

Comparing numbers

1 Copy the pairs of numbers. Write the correct symbol, > or <, between each pair.

- a 1111. 1101.
- b 1876. 1786.
- c 1232. 1223.
- d 1776. 1767.

REMEMBER < >

2 Write the number **1 more** than:
a 1427 b 1010 c 1101 d 1300.

3 Write the number **10 less** than:
a 1777 b 1234 c 1010 d 1000.

4 Write the number **100 more** than:
a 900 b 1325 c 1077 d 1566.

5 Write the number **1000 less** than:
a 1547 b 1999 c 1000 d 1010.

6 Write these numbers in order of size, largest first.

- a 1011 929 992 1101 1320 1232
- b 1092 1200 1000 1029 1220 1209

STEPS 3b:10 25

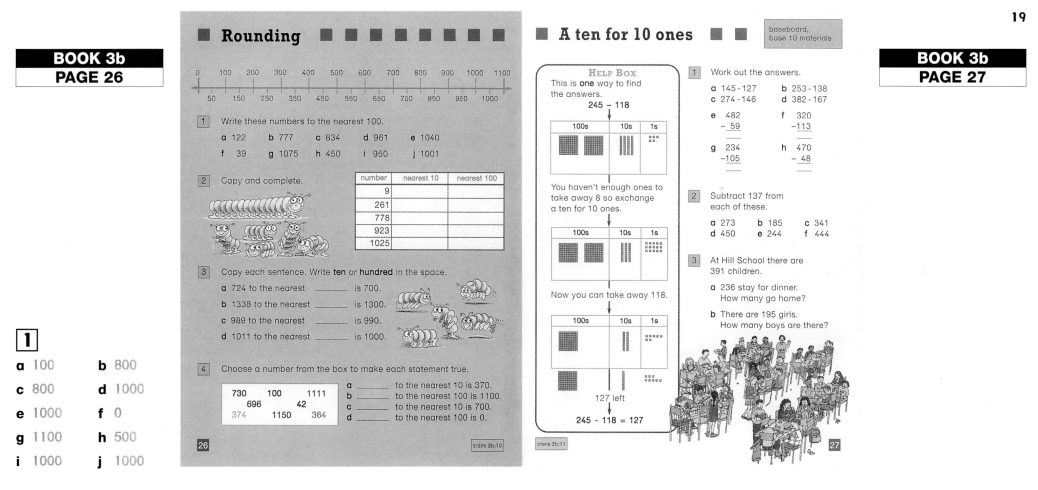

BOOK 3b
PAGE 26

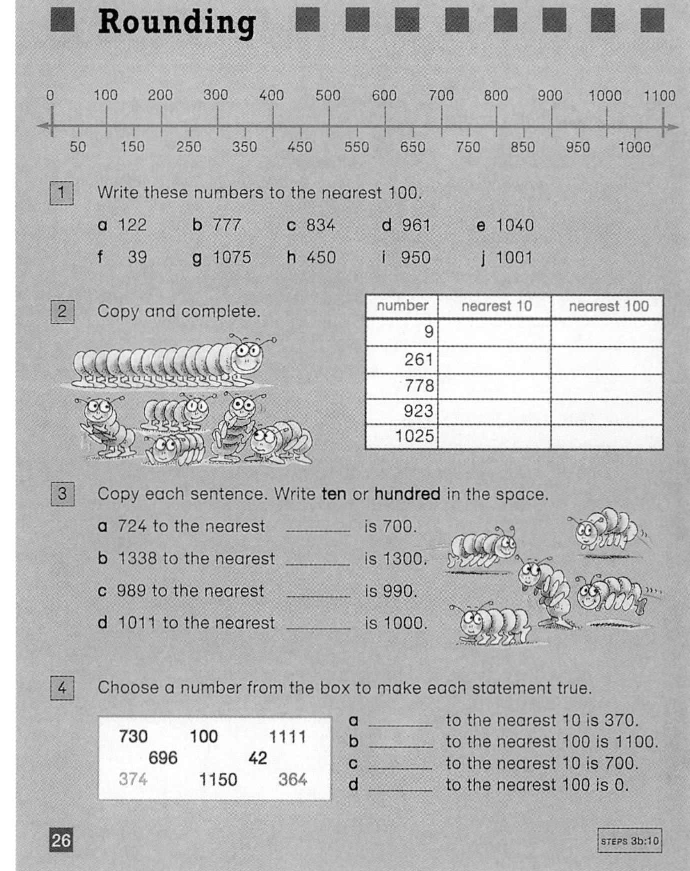

1

a 100 **b** 800
c 800 **d** 1000
e 1000 **f** 0
g 1100 **h** 500
i 1000 **j** 1000

2

number	nearest 10	nearest 100
9	10	0
261	260	300
778	780	800
923	920	900
1025	1030	1000

3

a 724 to the nearest hundred is 700.
b 1338 to the nearest hundred is 1300.
c 989 to the nearest ten is 990.
d 1011 to the nearest hundred is 1000.

4

a 374 to the nearest 10 is 370.
b 1111 to the nearest 100 is 1100.
c 696 to the nearest 10 is 700.
d 42 to the nearest 100 is 0.

BOOK 3b
PAGE 27

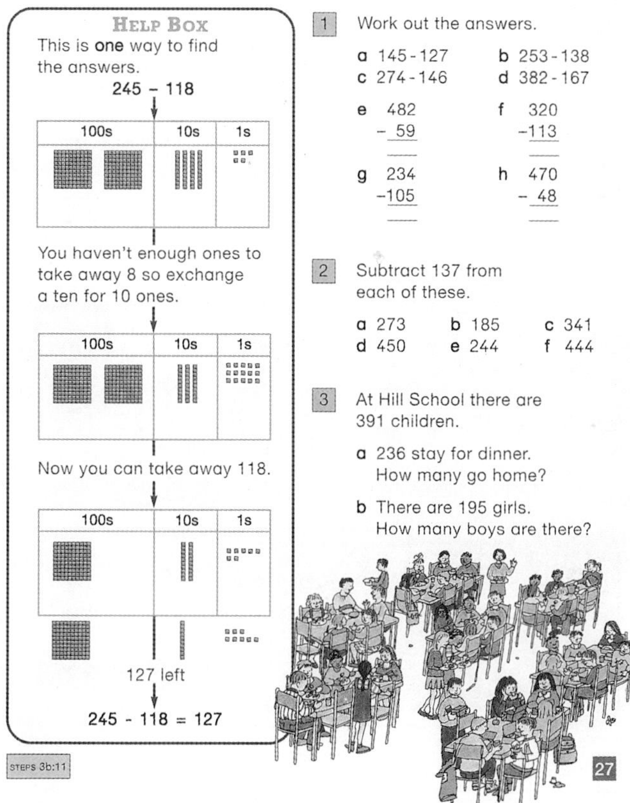

1

a 18 **b** 115 **c** 128 **d** 215 **e** 423 **f** 207 **g** 129 **h** 422

2

a 136 **b** 48 **c** 204 **d** 313 **e** 107 **f** 307

3

a 155 **b** 196

BOOK 3b
PAGE 28

More exchanging

1. Decide the best way to find the answers.

a 343 − 171 b 253 − 182 c 156 − 72

d	e	f
409 −236	327 −273	156 − 80

2. Subtract 163 from each of these.

a 234 b 258 c 306 d 415 e 327 f 409

3. Find the two subtractions that each have a mistake. Write them correctly.

a	b	c
405 − 72 333	346 − 64 382	274 −167 107

d	e	f
425 −372 53	290 − 47 243	341 −277 164

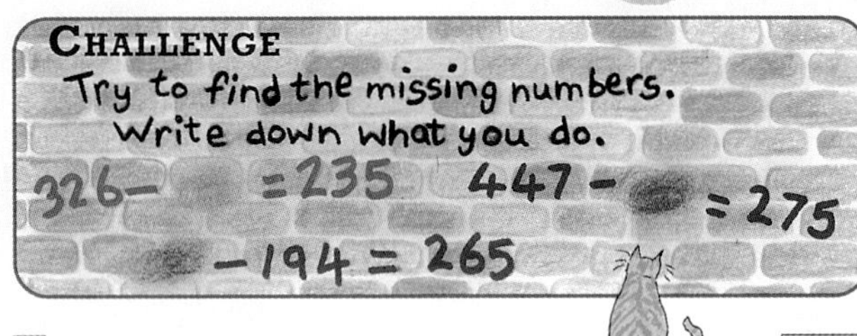

BOOK 3b
PAGE 29

Checking subtraction

baseboard, base 10 materials

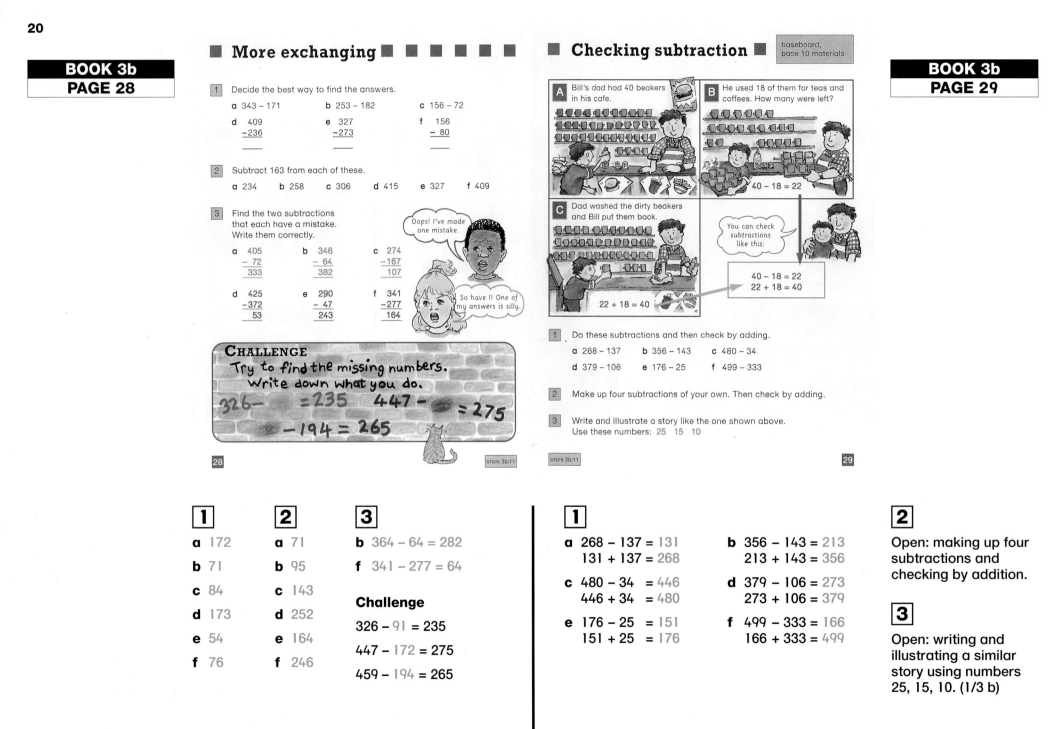

A Bill's dad had 40 beakers in his cafe.
B He used 18 of them for teas and coffees. How many were left?
40 − 18 = 22

C Dad washed the dirty beakers and Bill put them back.

22 + 18 = 40

You can check subtractions like this:

40 − 18 = 22
22 + 18 = 40

1. Do these subtractions and then check by adding.

a 268 − 137 b 356 − 143 c 480 − 34

d 379 − 106 e 176 − 25 f 499 − 333

2. Make up four subtractions of your own. Then check by adding.

3. Write and illustrate a story like the one shown above. Use these numbers: 25 15 10

1

a 172
b 71
c 84
d 173
e 54
f 76

2

a 71
b 95
c 143
d 252
e 164
f 246

3

b 364 − 64 = 282
f 341 − 277 = 64

Challenge

326 − 91 = 235
447 − 172 = 275
459 − 194 = 265

1

a 268 − 137 = 131
131 + 137 = 268

b 356 − 143 = 213
213 + 143 = 356

c 480 − 34 = 446
446 + 34 = 480

d 379 − 106 = 273
273 + 106 = 379

e 176 − 25 = 151
151 + 25 = 176

f 499 − 333 = 166
166 + 333 = 499

2

Open: making up four subtractions and checking by addition.

3

Open: writing and illustrating a similar story using numbers 25, 15, 10. (1/3 b)

BOOK 3b
PAGE 30

Colourful fractions

1 For each shape a to g, write the fraction that is coloured.

a b c d e f g

2 For each shape, a to g, write the fraction that is not coloured.

For shape a Sam wrote → $\frac{4}{5}$ is red. $\frac{1}{5}$ is white. $\frac{4}{5}+\frac{1}{5}=\frac{5}{5}=1$

3 Write about the shapes b to g in the same way as Sam.

What is the same about all of these? $\frac{4}{4}$ $\frac{5}{5}$ $\frac{6}{6}$ $\frac{7}{7}$ $\frac{8}{8}$ $\frac{10}{10}$

CHALLENGE

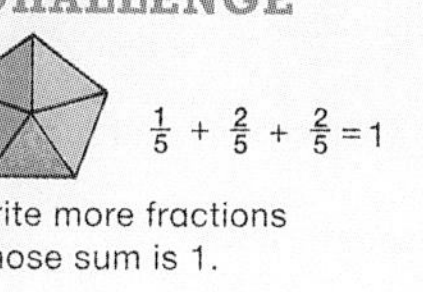

$\frac{1}{5}+\frac{2}{5}+\frac{2}{5}=1$

Write more fractions whose sum is 1.

30 STEPS 3b:12

Equal divisions

Paul drew a line 15 cm long. He divided it into 3 equal parts.

5cm 5cm 5cm

He wrote: $\frac{1}{3}$ of 15cm = 5cm ← is the same as → 15cm ÷ 3 = 5cm

1 Draw lines of these lengths. Divide them into 3 equal parts. Write about each one in the same way as Paul did.

a 6 cm b 9 cm c 12 cm

2 Draw lines of these lengths, Divide them into 4 equal parts. Write about each one in the same way.

a 8 cm b 16 cm c 20 cm

3 Choose 4 more lines to draw. Divide them into equal parts. Write about them in the same way.

4 Write a story about this picture.

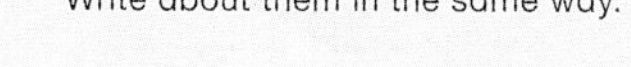

STEPS 3b:12 31

BOOK 3b
PAGE 31

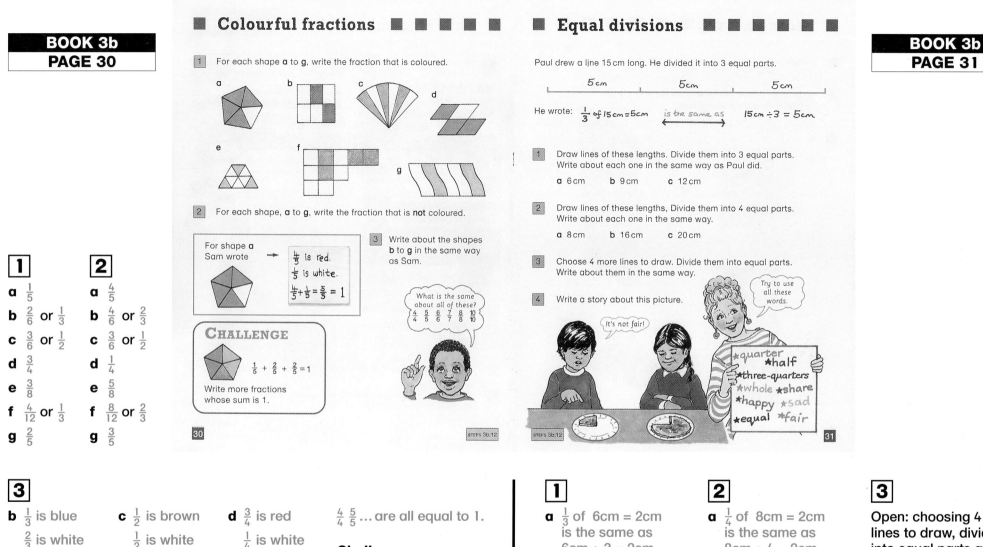

1

a $\frac{1}{5}$

b $\frac{2}{6}$ or $\frac{1}{3}$

c $\frac{3}{6}$ or $\frac{1}{2}$

d $\frac{3}{4}$

e $\frac{3}{8}$

f $\frac{4}{12}$ or $\frac{1}{3}$

g $\frac{2}{5}$

2

a $\frac{4}{5}$

b $\frac{4}{6}$ or $\frac{2}{3}$

c $\frac{3}{6}$ or $\frac{1}{2}$

d $\frac{1}{4}$

e $\frac{5}{8}$

f $\frac{8}{12}$ or $\frac{2}{3}$

g $\frac{3}{5}$

3

b $\frac{1}{3}$ is blue
$\frac{2}{3}$ is white
$\frac{1}{3}+\frac{2}{3}=1$

c $\frac{1}{2}$ is brown
$\frac{1}{2}$ is white
$\frac{1}{2}+\frac{1}{2}=1$

d $\frac{3}{4}$ is red
$\frac{1}{4}$ is white
$\frac{3}{4}+\frac{1}{4}=1$

e $\frac{3}{8}$ is yellow
$\frac{5}{8}$ is white
$\frac{3}{8}+\frac{5}{8}=1$

f $\frac{1}{3}$ is purple
$\frac{2}{3}$ is white
$\frac{1}{3}+\frac{2}{3}=1$

g $\frac{2}{5}$ is yellow
$\frac{3}{5}$ is white
$\frac{2}{5}+\frac{3}{5}=1$

$\frac{4}{4}$ $\frac{5}{5}$ ... are all equal to 1.

Challenge

Open: writing more fractions (all with the same denominator) whose sum is 1. (1/3b)

1

a $\frac{1}{3}$ of 6cm = 2cm is the same as 6cm ÷ 3 = 2cm

b $\frac{1}{3}$ of 9cm = 3cm is the same as 9cm ÷ 3 = 3cm

c $\frac{1}{3}$ of 12cm = 4cm is the same as 12cm ÷ 3 = 4cm

2

a $\frac{1}{4}$ of 8cm = 2cm is the same as 8cm ÷ 4 = 2cm

b $\frac{1}{4}$ of 16cm = 4cm is the same as 16cm ÷ 4 = 3cm

c $\frac{1}{4}$ of 20cm = 5cm is the same as 20cm ÷ 4 = 4cm

3

Open: choosing 4 more lines to draw, divide into equal parts and write about.

4

Open: write a story about the unfair sharing of a pizza. (1/3 a,b)

BOOK 3b PAGE 32

BOOK 3b PAGE 33

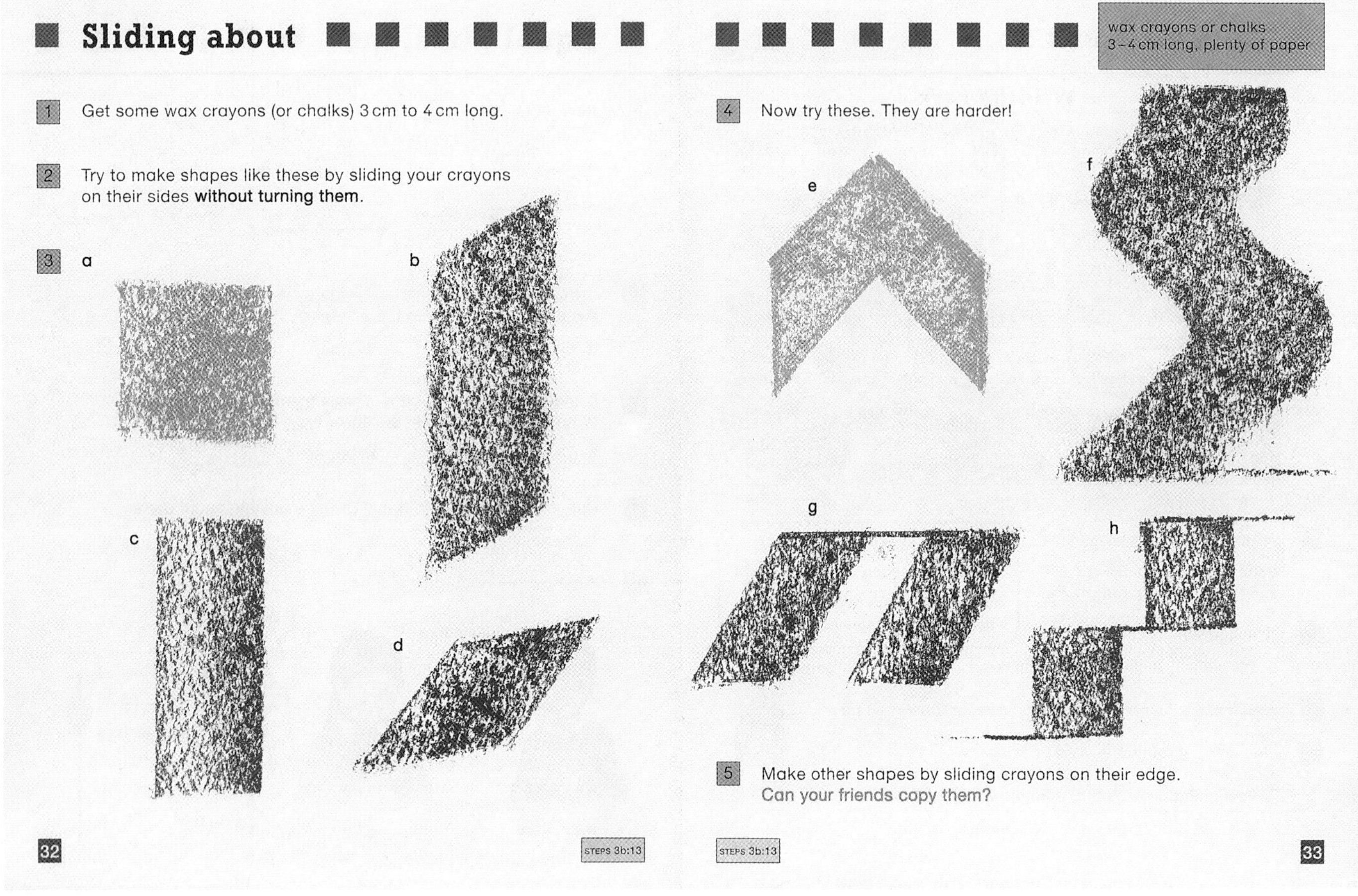

Sliding about
wax crayons or chalks 3–4 cm long, plenty of paper
1 Get some wax crayons (or chalks) 3 cm to 4 cm long.
2 Try to make shapes like these by sliding your crayons on their sides without turning them.
3 a
b
c
d
4 Now try these. They are harder!
e
f
g
h
5 Make other shapes by sliding crayons on their edge. Can your friends copy them?
32
STEPS 3b:13
STEPS 3b:13
33

1 – 3

Practical: sliding crayons on their sides to make:

a a square

b a parallelogram

c an oblong

d a rhombus

Practical: more difficult examples of previous exercise.

BOOK 3b
PAGE 34

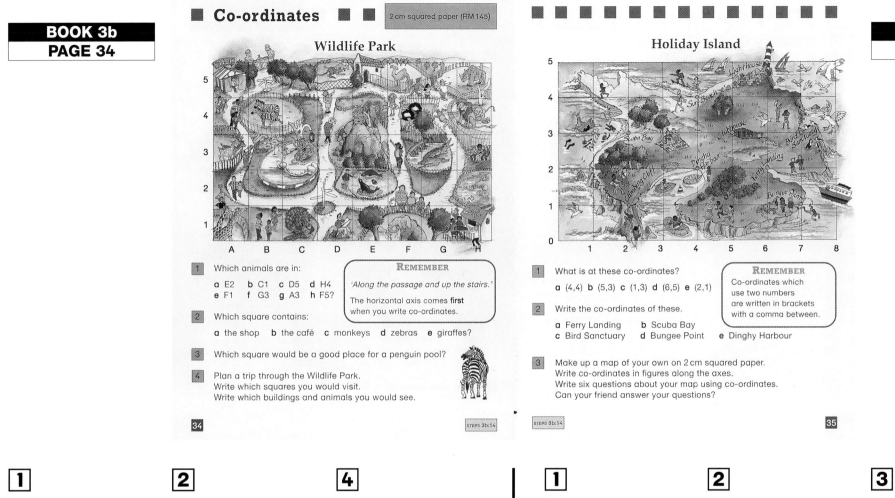

Co-ordinates

2 cm squared paper (RM 145)

Wildlife Park

1 Which animals are in:

a E2 b C1 c D5 d H4
e F1 f G3 g A3 h F5?

REMEMBER
'Along the passage and up the stairs.'
The horizontal axis comes **first** when you write co-ordinates.

2 Which square contains:

a the shop b the café c monkeys d zebras e giraffes?

3 Which square would be a good place for a penguin pool?

4 Plan a trip through the Wildlife Park.
Write which squares you would visit.
Write which buildings and animals you would see.

34 STEPS 3b:14

BOOK 3b
PAGE 35

Holiday Island

1 What is at these co-ordinates?

a (4,4) b (5,3) c (1,3) d (6,5) e (2,1)

REMEMBER
Co-ordinates which use two numbers are written in brackets with a comma between.

2 Write the co-ordinates of these.

a Ferry Landing b Scuba Bay
c Bird Sanctuary d Bungee Point e Dinghy Harbour

3 Make up a map of your own on 2 cm squared paper.
Write co-ordinates in figures along the axes.
Write six questions about your map using co-ordinates.
Can your friend answer your questions?

STEPS 3b:14 35

1

a seals
b peacocks
c kangaroos
d lions
e elephant
f crocodiles
g deer
h camel

2

a A5
b H1
c C3
d B4
e A1

3

H2

4

Open: planning a trip through the Wildlife Park listing squares visited and buildings and animals seen. (1/3 a,b,c)

1

a Surfbeach
b Clubhouse
c Wreck
d Lighthouse
e Climbing Cliff

2

a (6,2)
b (2,3)
c (7,3)
d (7,1)
e (4,2)

3

Practical: making own map with co-ordinates and questions to be answered.

BOOK 3b
PAGE 36

BOOK 3b
PAGE 37

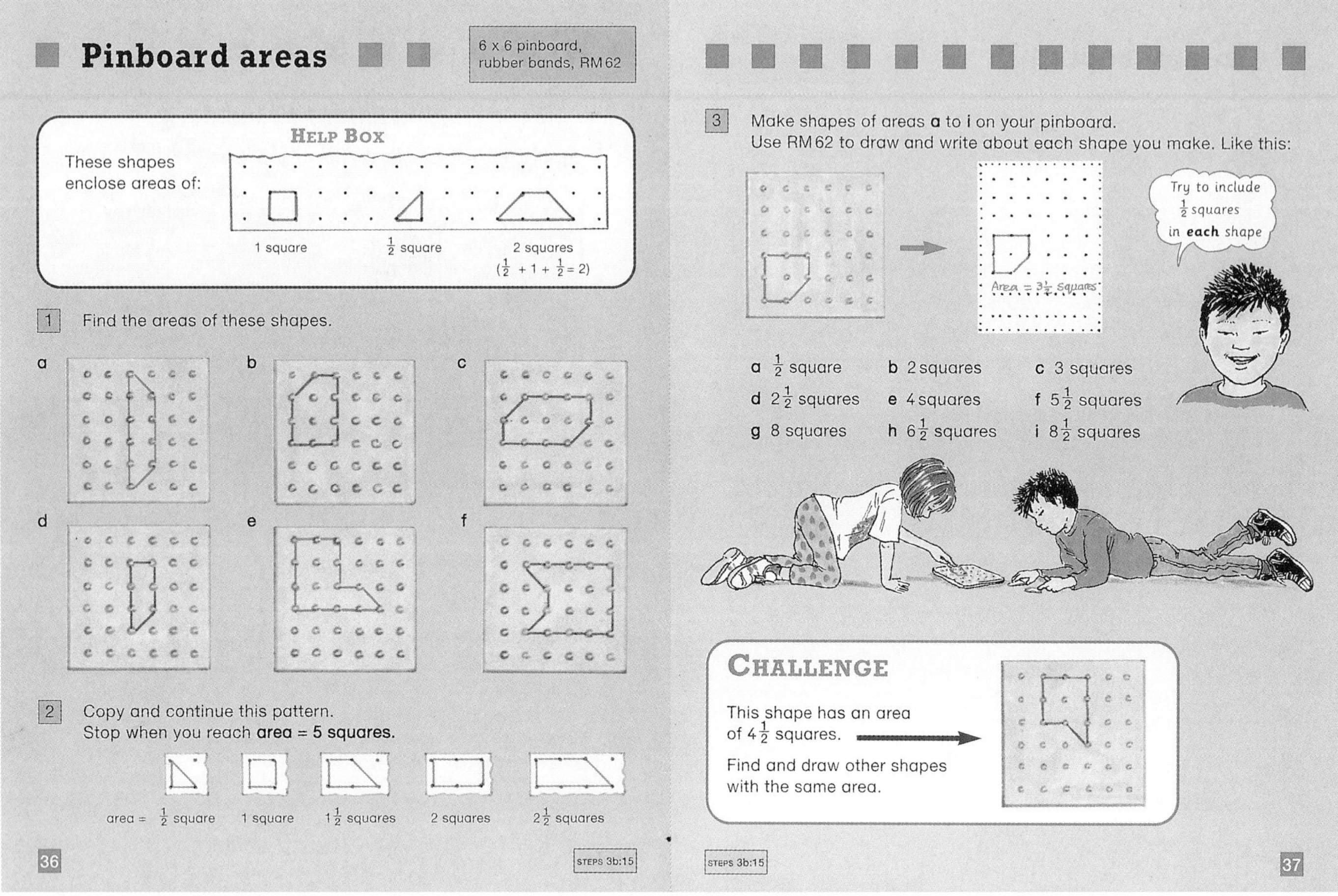

Pinboard areas

6 x 6 pinboard, rubber bands, RM 62

HELP BOX

These shapes enclose areas of:

1 square — $\frac{1}{2}$ square — 2 squares ($\frac{1}{2} + 1 + \frac{1}{2} = 2$)

1 Find the areas of these shapes.

a b c d e f

2 Copy and continue this pattern. Stop when you reach **area = 5 squares**.

area = $\frac{1}{2}$ square, 1 square, $1\frac{1}{2}$ squares, 2 squares, $2\frac{1}{2}$ squares

36 STEPS 3b:15

3 Make shapes of areas **a** to **i** on your pinboard. Use RM 62 to draw and write about each shape you make. Like this:

Area = $3\frac{1}{2}$ squares

Try to include $\frac{1}{2}$ squares in **each** shape

a $\frac{1}{2}$ square	b 2 squares	c 3 squares
d $2\frac{1}{2}$ squares	e 4 squares	f $5\frac{1}{2}$ squares
g 8 squares	h $6\frac{1}{2}$ squares	i $8\frac{1}{2}$ squares

CHALLENGE

This shape has an area of $4\frac{1}{2}$ squares.

Find and draw other shapes with the same area.

STEPS 3b:15 37

1

a 4 squares

b $5\frac{1}{2}$ squares

c 7 squares

d $2\frac{1}{2}$ squares

e $7\frac{1}{2}$ squares

f 10 squares

2

Practical: copying and continuing a pattern of areas, increasing by $\frac{1}{2}$ square each time, as far as an area of 5 squares. (1/3 a,c)

3

Practical: making shapes of areas:

a $\frac{1}{2}$ square	**b** 2 squares	**c** 3 squares
d $2\frac{1}{2}$ squares	**e** 4 squares	**f** $5\frac{1}{2}$ squares
g 8 squares	**h** $6\frac{1}{2}$ squares	**i** $8\frac{1}{2}$ squares

and trying to include $\frac{1}{2}$ squares in each shape.

Challenge

Find and draw other shapes with an area of $4\frac{1}{2}$ squares. (1/3 b,c)

BOOK 3b
PAGE 38

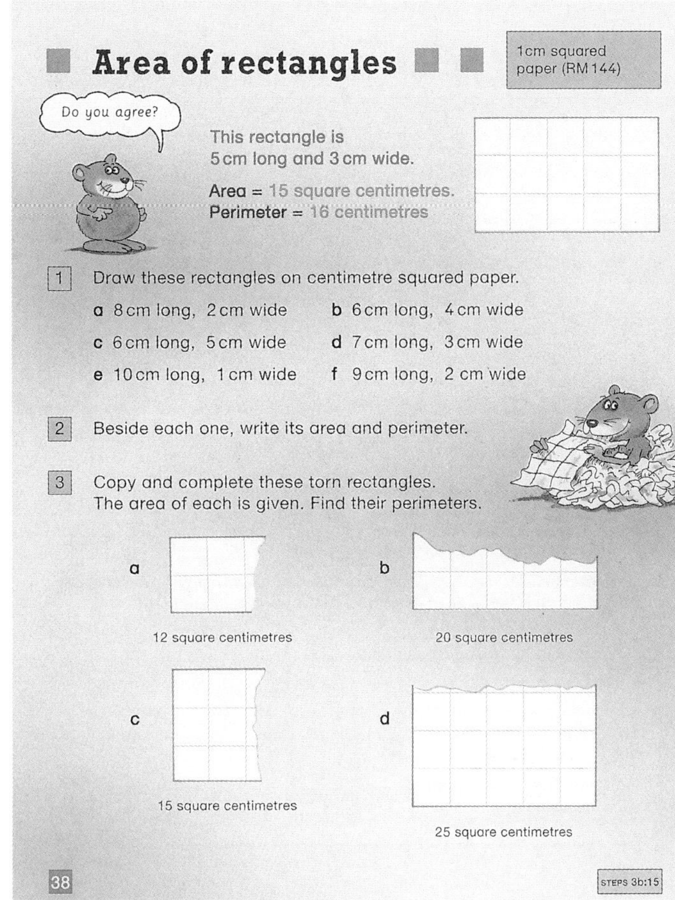

Area of rectangles

1cm squared paper (RM 144)

Do you agree?

This rectangle is 5 cm long and 3 cm wide.

Area = 15 square centimetres.
Perimeter = 16 centimetres

1 Draw these rectangles on centimetre squared paper.

a 8 cm long, 2 cm wide
b 6 cm long, 4 cm wide
c 6 cm long, 5 cm wide
d 7 cm long, 3 cm wide
e 10 cm long, 1 cm wide
f 9 cm long, 2 cm wide

2 Beside each one, write its area and perimeter.

3 Copy and complete these torn rectangles. The area of each is given. Find their perimeters.

a 12 square centimetres
b 20 square centimetres
c 15 square centimetres
d 25 square centimetres

38 STEPS 3b:15

Practical: drawing rectangles on centimetre squared paper.

2

a 8cm by 2cm
area 16 square centimetres
perimeter 20 centimetres

b 6cm by 4cm
area 24 square centimetres
perimeter 20 centimetres

c 6cm by 5cm
area 30 square centimetres
perimeter 22 centimetres

d 7cm by 3cm
area 21 square centimetres
perimeter 20 centimetres

e 10cm by 1cm
area 10 square centimetres
perimeter 22 centimetres

f 9cm by 2cm
area 18 square centimetres
perimeter 22 centimetres

3

a Perimeter 16cm

b Perimeter 18cm

c Perimeter 16cm

d Perimeter 20cm

BOOK 3b
PAGE 39

Balancing weights

balance scales, rice, plastic bag

These are standard weights up to 500g.

1g 5g 10g 20g 50g 100g 200g 500g

1 Write five ways to balance 50g using these standard weights.

2 Use scales and a plastic bag. Weigh out 70g of rice into a bag. Label the bag.

70g

3 Write five ways to balance 70g of rice using the weights shown above.

4 Copy and complete.

a Three standard weights which balance 500g are ____ g and ____ g and ____ g.

b Four standard weights which balance 130g are ____ g and ____ g and ____ g and ____ g.

CHALLENGE

Use **only** balance scales, a 20g weight and Plasticine.
Work out ways to make lumps of Plasticine which weigh:

a 80g b 50g c 10g d 40g e 25g f 5g

STEPS 3b:16 39

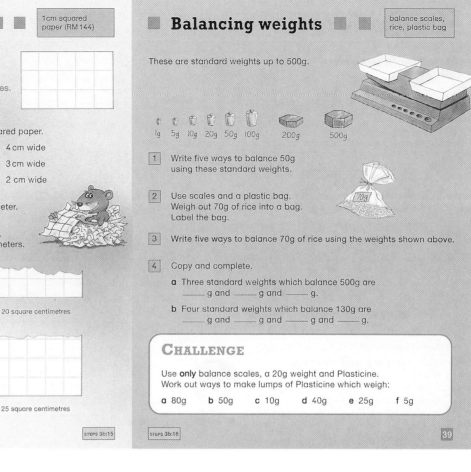

1 Open: finding five ways to balance 50g using the weights listed in 1:
For example: 50 g; (20 g + 20 g + 10 g); (20 g + 10 g + 10 g + 5 g + 5 g); etc.

2 Practical: weighing out 70 g of rice in a bag and labelling it. (1/3 a)

3 Open: finding five ways to balance 70 g using the weights listed in 1:
For example:
(50 g + 20 g); (50 g + 10 g + 5 g + 5 g); etc.

4

a Three standard weights which balance 500 g are 200 g and 200 g and 100 g.

b Four standard weights which balance 130 g are 100 g and 10 g and 10 g and 10 g or 50 g and 50 g and 20 g and 10 g, etc. (1/3 a)

Challenge

a Weigh out 4 lots of 20 g of Plasticine and roll them together to make 80 g.

b Weigh out 3 lots of 20 g, halve one of them to make two 10 g lumps and join 20 g + 20 g + 10 g to make 50 g.

c Weigh out 20 g and halve it by balancing 10 g against 10 g.

d Weigh out 2 lots of 20 g, combine them to make 40 g.

e Halve the 50 g made in **b** or combine 20 g and half of half of 20 g.

f Halve 20 g and halve one 10 g lump to make 5 g.

BOOK 3b
PAGE 40

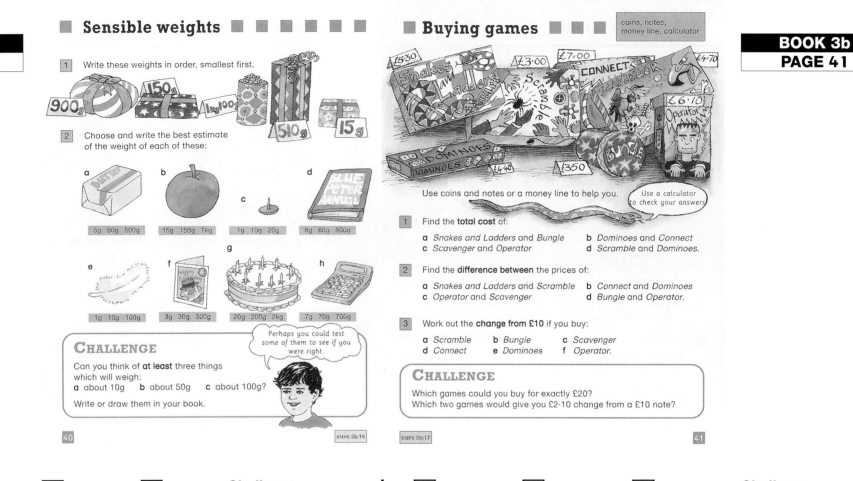

Sensible weights

1 Write these weights in order, smallest first.

2 Choose and write the best estimate of the weight of each of these:

a 5g 50g 500g

b 15g 150g 1kg

c 1g 10g 20g

d 8g 80g 800g

e 1g 10g 100g

f 3g 30g 300g

g 20g 200g 2kg

h 7g 70g 700g

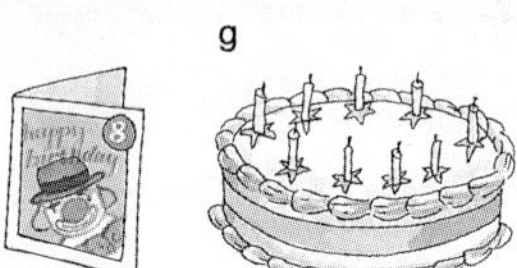

CHALLENGE

Perhaps you could test some of them to see if you were right.

Can you think of **at least** three things which will weigh:
a about 10g b about 50g c about 100g?

Write or draw them in your book.

40 STEPS 2b:16

BOOK 3b
PAGE 41

Buying games

Use coins and notes or a money line to help you.

Use a calculator to check your answers.

1 Find the **total cost** of:

a *Snakes and Ladders* and *Bungle*
b *Dominoes* and *Connect*
c *Scavenger* and *Operator*
d *Scramble* and *Dominoes*.

2 Find the **difference between** the prices of:

a *Snakes and Ladders* and *Scramble*
b *Connect* and *Dominoes*
c *Operator* and *Scavenger*
d *Bungle* and *Operator*.

3 Work out the **change from £10** if you buy:

a *Scramble* b *Bungle* c *Scavenger*
d *Connect* e *Dominoes* f *Operator*.

CHALLENGE

Which games could you buy for exactly £20?
Which two games would give you £2·10 change from a £10 note?

STEPS 3b:17 41

Book 3b Page 40 answers

1

a 15 g
150 g
510 g
900 g
1 kg 100 g

2

a 50 g
b 150 g
c 1 g
d 800 g
e 1 g
f 40 g
g 2 kg
h 70 g

Challenge

Open: find at least things which weigh:

a about 100 g
b about 50 g
c about 500 g

Book 3b Page 41 answers

1

a £8.80
b £11.40
c £10.80
d £7.40

2

a £2.30
b £2.60
c £1.40
d £2.60

3

a £7.00
b £6.50
c £5.30
d £3.00
e £5.60
f £2.90

Challenge

Snakes and Ladders, Scavenger, Scramble and Connect cost £20.

Dominoes and Bungle cost £7.90 (£2.10 change from a £10 note).

BOOK 3b
PAGE 42

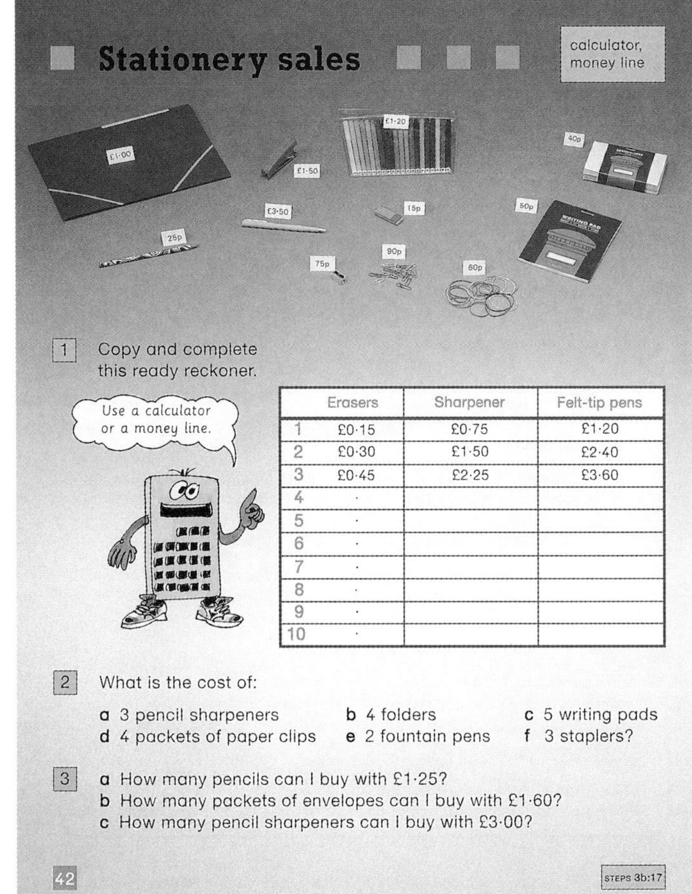

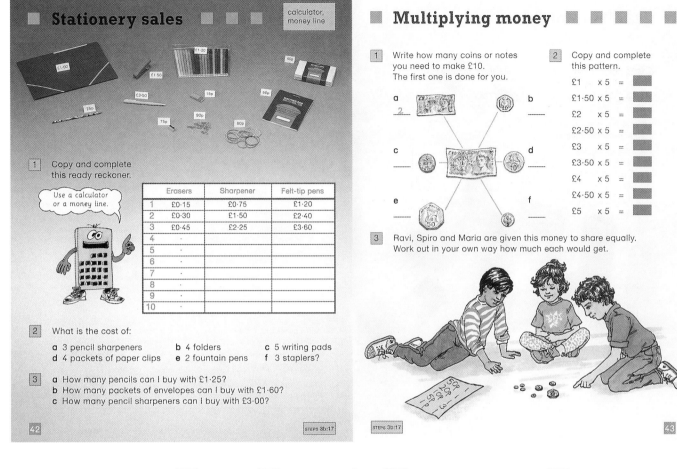

Stationery sales

calculator, money line

1 Copy and complete this ready reckoner.

	Erasers	Sharpener	Felt-tip pens
1	£0·15	£0·75	£1·20
2	£0·30	£1·50	£2·40
3	£0·45	£2·25	£3·60
4	·		
5	·		
6	·		
7	·		
8	·		
9	·		
10	·		

2 What is the cost of:

a 3 pencil sharpeners b 4 folders c 5 writing pads
d 4 packets of paper clips e 2 fountain pens f 3 staplers?

3 a How many pencils can I buy with £1·25?
b How many packets of envelopes can I buy with £1·60?
c How many pencil sharpeners can I buy with £3·00?

Multiplying money

BOOK 3b
PAGE 43

1 Write how many coins or notes you need to make £10.
The first one is done for you.

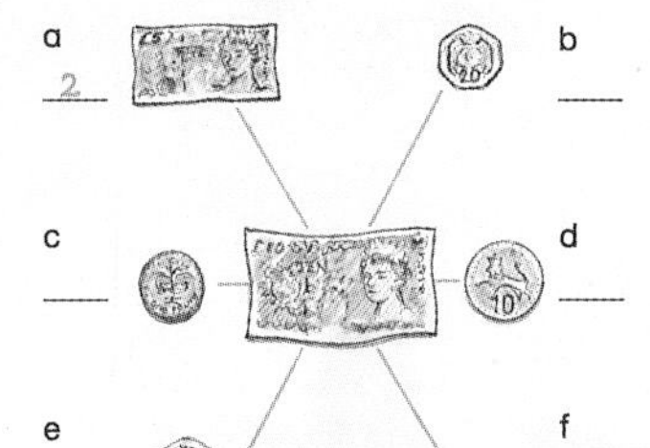

a 2
b ____
c ____
d ____
e ____
f ____

2 Copy and complete this pattern.

£1 x 5 =
£1·50 x 5 =
£2 x 5 =
£2·50 x 5 =
£3 x 5 =
£3·50 x 5 =
£4 x 5 =
£4·50 x 5 =
£5 x 5 =

3 Ravi, Spiro and Maria are given this money to share equally.
Work out in your own way how much each would get.

1

	Eraser	Sharpener	Felt-tip pens
1	£0.15	£0.75	£1.20
2	£0.30	£1.50	£2.40
3	£0.45	£2.25	£3.60
4	£0.60	£3.00	£4.80
5	£0.75	£3.75	£6.00
6	£0.90	£4.50	£7.20
7	£1.05	£5.25	£8.40
8	£1.20	£6.00	£9.60
9	£1.35	£6.75	£10.80
10	£1.50	£7.50	£12.00

2

a £2.25
b £4.00
c £2.50
d £3.60
e £7.00
f £4.50

3

a 5
b 4
c 4

1

b 50
c 1000
d 100
e 20
f 200

2

£1 x 5 = £5.00
£1.50 x 5 = £7.50
£2 x 5 = £10.00
£2.50 x 5 = £12.50
£3 x 5 = £15.00
£3.50 x 5 = £17.50
£4 x 5 = £20.00
£4.50 x 5 = £22.50
£5 x 5 = £25.00

3

32p

BOOK 3b
PAGE 44

Cube volumes

interlocking cubes

1 Make this shape.

a How many cubes have you used?

b What is the volume of the shape?

c Make five different shapes with the same volume.

2 Make these shapes. Write which pairs of shapes have the **same volume.**

44 STEPS 3b:18

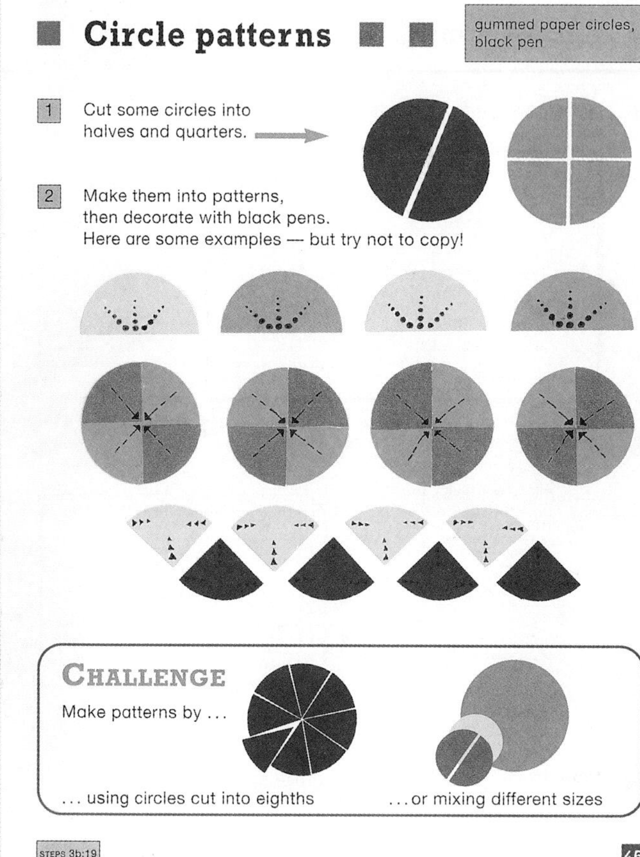

Circle patterns

gummed paper circles, black pen

1 Cut some circles into halves and quarters.

2 Make them into patterns, then decorate with black pens. Here are some examples — but try not to copy!

CHALLENGE

Make patterns by . . .

. . . using circles cut into eighths

. . .or mixing different sizes

STEPS 3b:19 45

BOOK 3b
PAGE 45

1

a 4

b 4 cubes

c Practical: making five different shapes with volume of 4 cubes.

2

Practical: making shapes shown.

a and **c** have the same volume

b and **d** have the same volume

1 **2**

Practical: making patterns with half and quarter circles.

Challenge

Making patterns using eighths of circles or different sizes of circles.
(1/3 a)

BOOK 3b
PAGE 46

BOOK 3b
PAGE 47

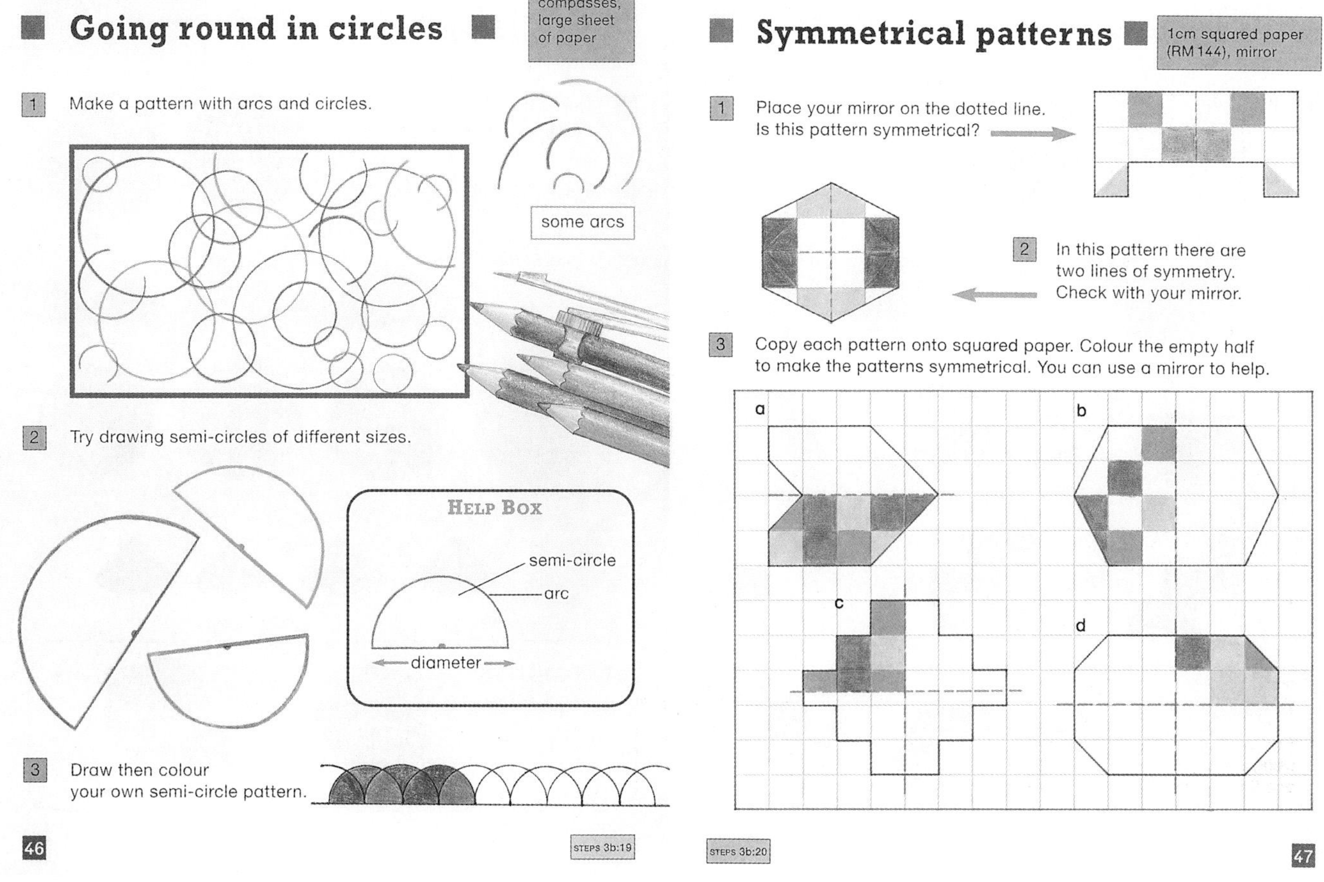

Going round in circles
compasses, large sheet of paper
1 Make a pattern with arcs and circles.
some arcs
2 Try drawing semi-circles of different sizes.
HELP BOX
semi-circle
arc
diameter
3 Draw then colour your own semi-circle pattern.
46
STEPS 3b:19
Symmetrical patterns
1cm squared paper (RM 144), mirror
1 Place your mirror on the dotted line. Is this pattern symmetrical?
2 In this pattern there are two lines of symmetry. Check with your mirror.
3 Copy each pattern onto squared paper. Colour the empty half to make the patterns symmetrical. You can use a mirror to help.
a
b
c
d
STEPS 3b:20
47

1 – 3

Practical: making patterns with arcs, circles and semi-circles.

1 2

Practical: using a mirror to check symmetry.

3

Practical: copying and completing symmetrical patterns onto squared paper.

BOOK 3b
PAGE 48

Symmetry puzzle

mirror

1 Use a mirror on this shape to find shapes **a** to **h**.

a b c d e f g h

CHALLENGE

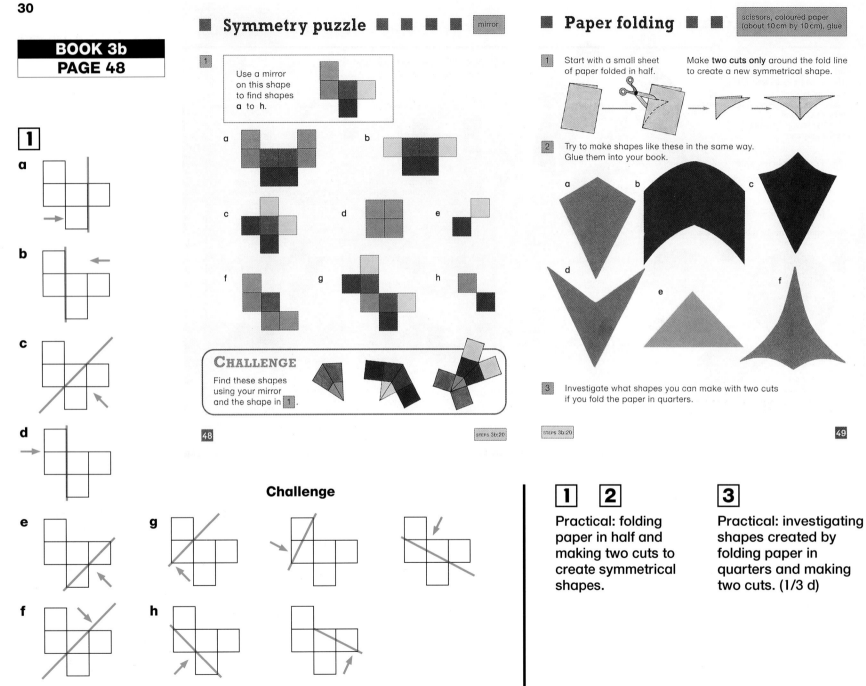

Find these shapes using your mirror and the shape in 1.

Paper folding

scissors, coloured paper (about 10 cm by 10 cm), glue

1 Start with a small sheet of paper folded in half. Make **two cuts only** around the fold line to create a new symmetrical shape.

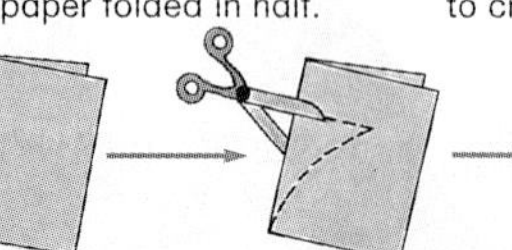

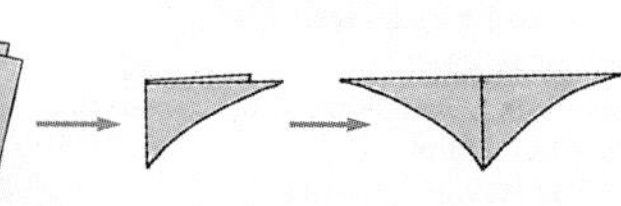

2 Try to make shapes like these in the same way. Glue them into your book.

3 Investigate what shapes you can make with two cuts if you fold the paper in quarters.

BOOK 3b
PAGE 49

1

a

b

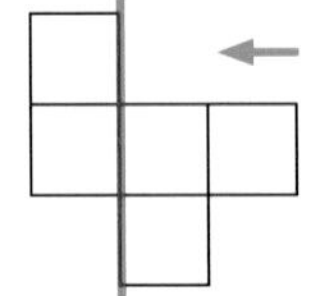

c

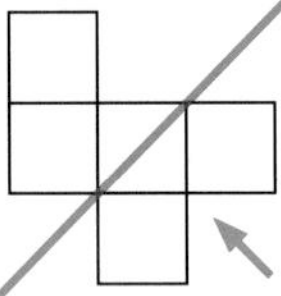

d

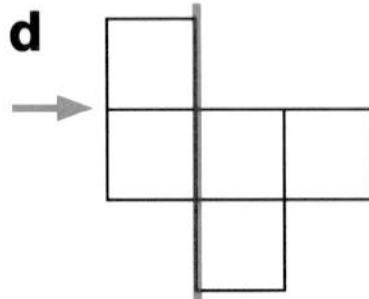

e

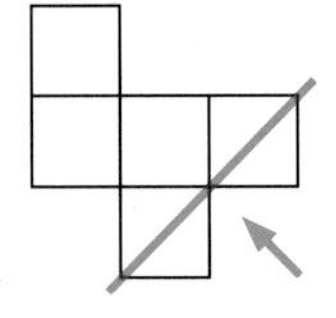

f

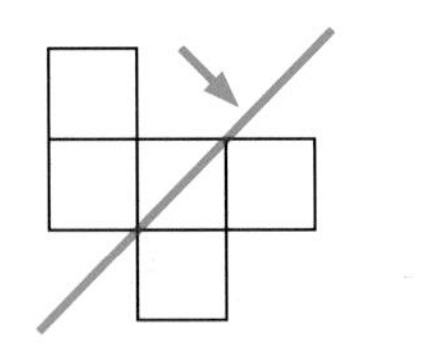

g

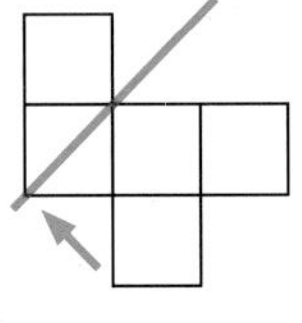

h

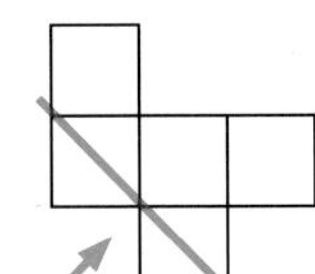

Challenge

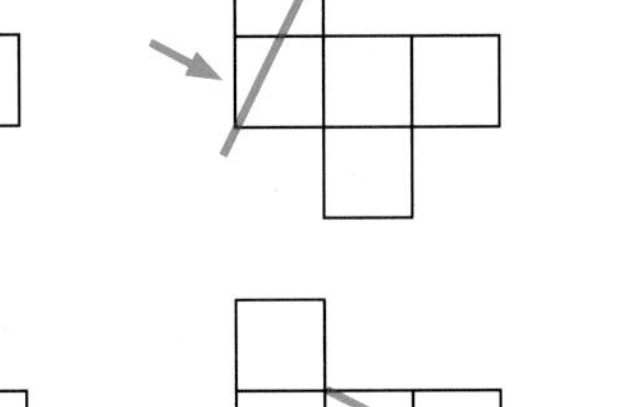

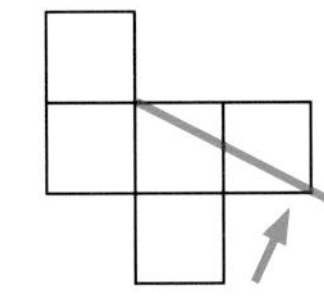

1 **2**

Practical: folding paper in half and making two cuts to create symmetrical shapes.

3

Practical: investigating shapes created by folding paper in quarters and making two cuts. (1/3 d)

BOOK 3b
PAGE 50

What's the chance?

Jimmy, Ela, Morag and Gary are playing a game. They take turns to spin a colour spinner. If they spin the colour of their T-shirts, they win a point. The first to win 4 points wins the game.

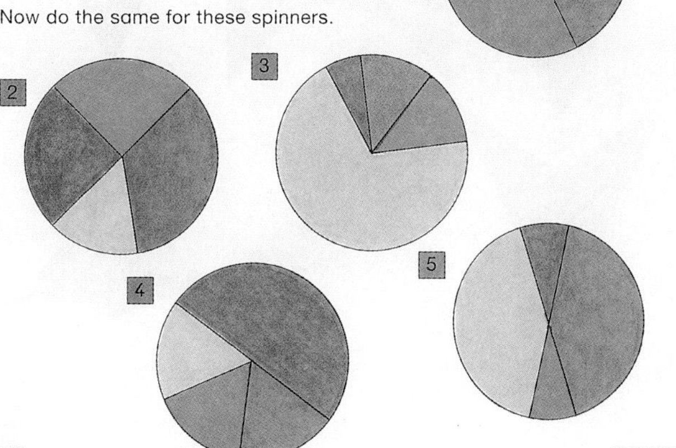

1 For this spinner, write:

a who has the best chance of winning?
b who has the poorest chance of winning?
c which players have an equal chance of winning?

Now do the same for these spinners.

2

3

4

5

coloured stickers, blank dice

BOOK 3b
PAGE 51

6 Design two more spinners, **a** and **b**.

Spinner **a**: Each player has an **equal** chance of winning.

Spinner **b**: Jimmy and Ela have a **good** chance of winning but Morag and Gary have a **poor** chance.

7 Use stickers in two colours and a blank dice.

1 Make a dice using both colours, one sticker on each face.
2 Predict how many times each colour will occur in 60 rolls.
3 Write down your prediction.
4 Make 60 rolls and, each time, keep a note of the colour. (Choose your own way to do this).
5 Afterwards, write the total number of rolls for each colour.
Was your prediction nearly right?

What if we used 3 colours of stickers instead?

1

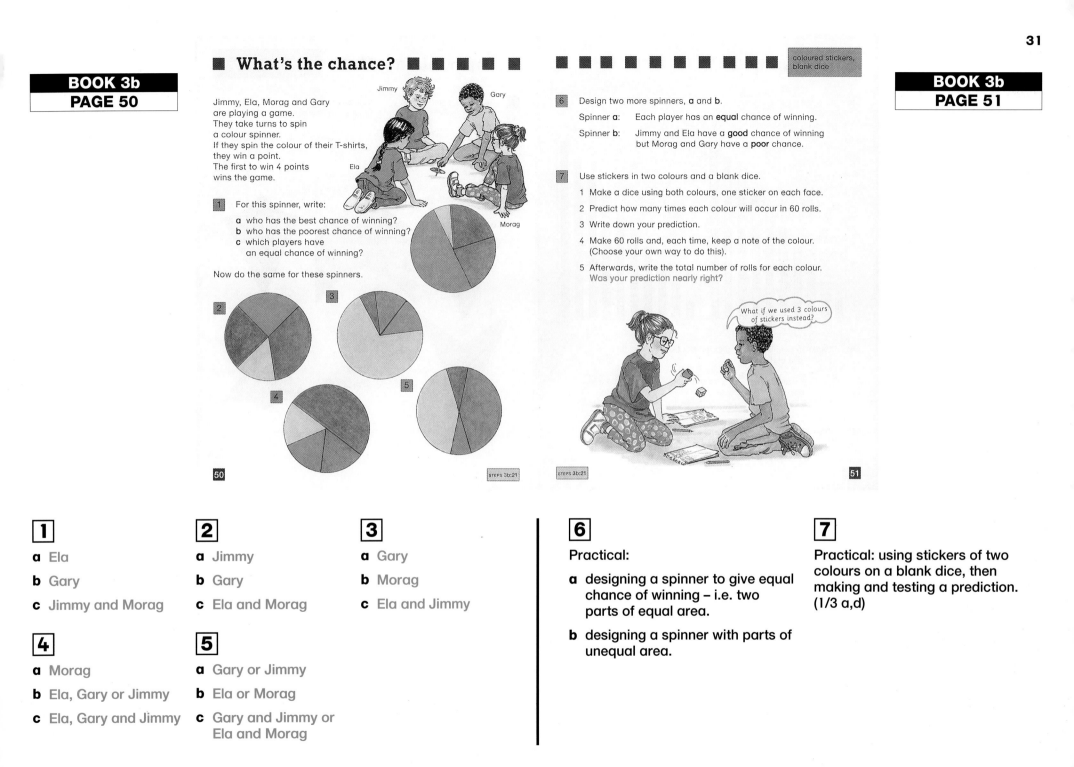

a Ela
b Gary
c Jimmy and Morag

2

a Jimmy
b Gary
c Ela and Morag

3

a Gary
b Morag
c Ela and Jimmy

4

a Morag
b Ela, Gary or Jimmy
c Ela, Gary and Jimmy

5

a Gary or Jimmy
b Ela or Morag
c Gary and Jimmy or Ela and Morag

6

Practical:

a designing a spinner to give equal chance of winning – i.e. two parts of equal area.
b designing a spinner with parts of unequal area.

7

Practical: using stickers of two colours on a blank dice, then making and testing a prediction. (1/3 a,d)

BOOK 3b
PAGE 52

Table graphs

Lucy drew this graph showing the '2 x' and 'x 2' tables.

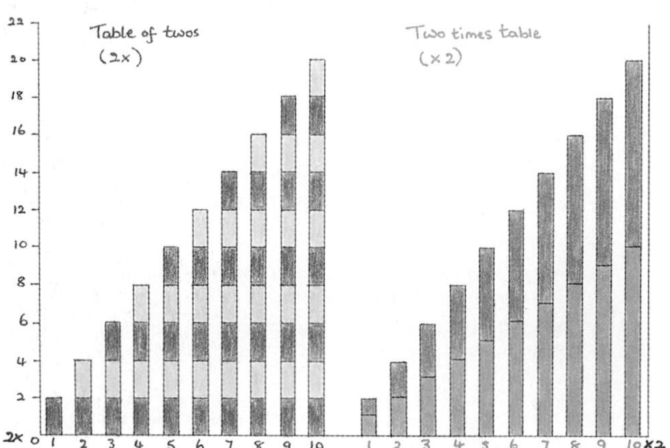

1 Choose materials to draw a graph like Lucy's to show **one** of these.

a 'x 3' table and '3 x' table or b 'x 4' table and '4 x' table or c 'x 5' table and '5 x' table

2 Now work out which answers are in both the 'x 2' table and the table you drew. Show how you do this.

52 STEPS 3b:22

Multiplication

calculator, completed copy of RM 89

BOOK 3b
PAGE 53

1 Copy and complete.

a 3 x 5 = ___	b 9 x ___ = 18	c 7 x ___ = 14
d ___ x 4 = 16	e 10 x 7 = ___	f ___ x 10 = 100
g ___ x 9 = 90	h 7 x ___ = 35	i 4 x 4 = ___

2 Find at least 5 different answers between 10 and 50 to each of these.

a ___ x 2 = ___ b 5 x ___ = ___ c ___ x 10 = ___

3 Use your grid on RM 89 to help you answer these.

a 7 x 8 = ___	b 9 x 6 = ___
c 6 x ___ = 48	d ___ x 8 = 32
e ___ x 7 = 49	f ___ x 9 = 63
g 9 x ___ = 81	h ___ x 5 = 45

Try to work out the answer to 3 in your head first.

CHALLENGE

Write down how you work out the answers.

Try to do these without the help of materials or your teacher.

a 13 x 5 = ___ b 5 x 16 = ___
c 15 x 6 = ___ d 25 x 9 = ___

STEPS 3b:22 53

Challenge

a 13 x 5 = 65
b 5 x 16 = 80
c 15 x 6 = 90
d 25 x 9 = 225

1

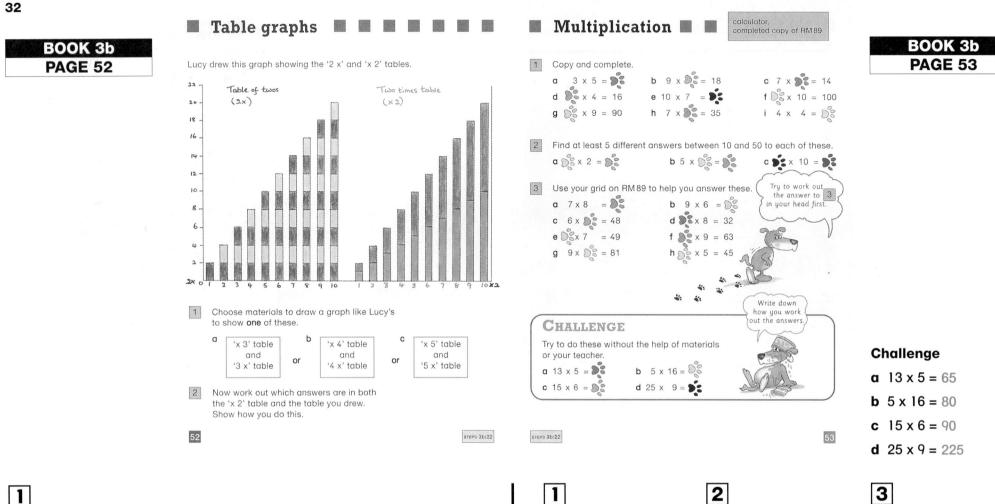

Practical: drawing graphs of either **a** 3, **b** 4 or **c** 5 times table.

2

If **a** chosen: 6, 12, 18, 24, . . .
If **b** chosen: 4, 8, 12, 16, 20, . . .
If **c** chosen: 10, 20, 30, . . .

1

a 3 x 5 = 15
b 9 x 2 = 18
c 7 x 2 = 14
d 4 x 4 = 16
e 10 x 7 = 70
f 10 x 10 = 100
g 10 x 9 = 90
h 7 x 5 = 35
i 4 x 4 = 16

2

Open: finding at least 5 different answers between 10 and 50 for each of:
a multiplication by 2
b multiplication by 5
c multiplication by 10.
(1/3 a)

3

a 7 x 8 = 56
b 9 x 6 = 54
c 6 x 8 = 48
d 4 x 8 = 32
e 7 x 7 = 49
f 7 x 9 = 63
g 9 x 9 = 81
h 9 x 5 = 45

BOOK 3b
PAGE 54

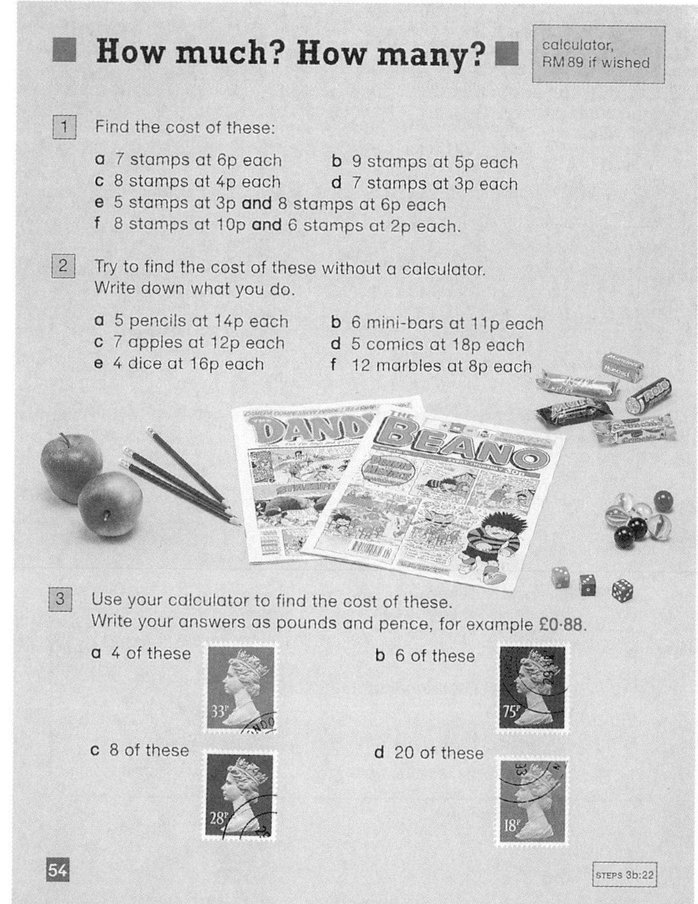

How much? How many?

calculator, RM 89 if wished

1 Find the cost of these:

a 7 stamps at 6p each
b 9 stamps at 5p each
c 8 stamps at 4p each
d 7 stamps at 3p each
e 5 stamps at 3p **and** 8 stamps at 6p each
f 8 stamps at 10p **and** 6 stamps at 2p each.

2 Try to find the cost of these without a calculator. Write down what you do.

a 5 pencils at 14p each
b 6 mini-bars at 11p each
c 7 apples at 12p each
d 5 comics at 18p each
e 4 dice at 16p each
f 12 marbles at 8p each

3 Use your calculator to find the cost of these. Write your answers as pounds and pence, for example £0·88.

a 4 of these (33p)
b 6 of these (75p)
c 8 of these (28p)
d 20 of these (18p)

54 STEPS 3b:22

BOOK 3b
PAGE 55

Split and multiply

straw

Here are 10 rows of 5 stickers.

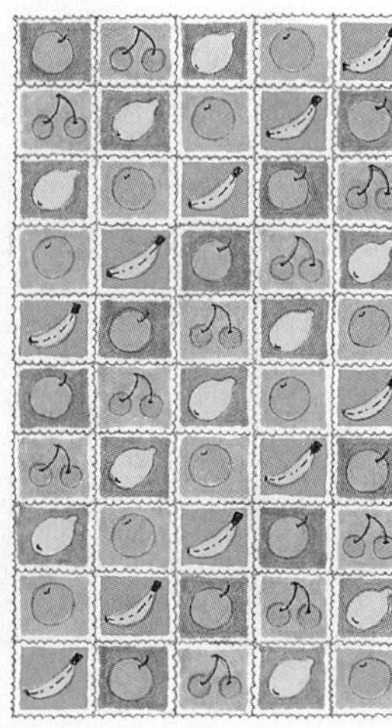

5 x 10 = 50

1 Use your straw to split the block of stickers into 6 rows and 4 rows.

2 Now split the stickers in each of these ways. Write about each one.

a 5 rows and 5 rows
b 3 rows and 7 rows
c 8 rows and 2 rows
d 1 row and 9 rows

3 Draw six more boxes like this to show different ways of splitting groups of two.

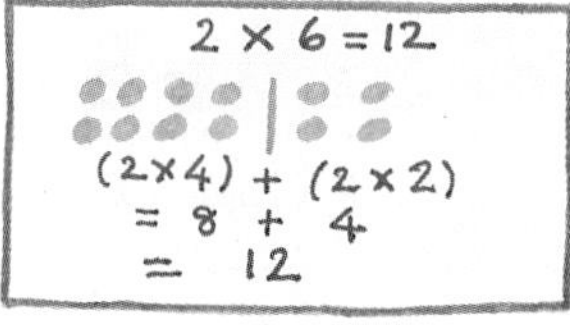

STEPS 3b:22 55

1

a 42p b 45p c 32p d 21p e 63p f 92p

2

a 70p b 66p c 84p d 90p e 64p f 96p

3

a £1.32 b £4.50 c £2.44 d £3.60

1

Practical: dividing 10 rows of 5 into 6 rows of 5 and 4 rows of 5.

2

a (5x5)+(5x5)
= 25 + 25
= 50

b (5x3)+(5x7)
= 15 + 35
= 50

c (5x8)+(5x2)
= 40 + 10
= 50

d (5x1)+(5x9)
= 5 + 45
= 50

3

Open: drawing diagrams to show 6 different ways of splitting groups of 2.
(1/3 b,c)

BOOK 3b
PAGE 56

Writing decimals

1 Write in **decimal form** how much is coloured.

a b c d e

2 Write these in decimal form.

a 2 units and 2 tenths b 0·9 and 3 units c 2·0 and $\frac{5}{10}$

d six tenths and 0 units e $\frac{7}{10}$ and 1 unit f 2 units and 0 tenths

3 0 1 2 3

Write these decimals in order of size, **smallest** first.

a 2·2	1·9	0·7	1·2	2·6
b 1·1	0·9	1·3	0·3	1.2
c 2·4	2·0	3·0	2·7	2.5

CHALLENGE

a Fit these digits 1 3 4 into these frames □□·□ to make 6 different decimal numbers.

b Then put the numbers in order of size, **largest** first.

56 STEPS 3b:23

BOOK 3b
PAGE 57

Adding decimals

base 10 materials, decimal abacus, RM95, calculator

Choose materials to help you with 1 and 2.

1 Add these decimals.

a 0·3 + 1·3	b 2·6 + 0·7	c 4·8 + 1·7
d 2·8 + 4·2	e 6·9 + 1·7	f 3·3 + 6·6
g 2·5 + 4·5	h 5·7 + 0·9	i 3·2 + 4·9

2 Find at least 5 pairs of numbers which total 2·4.

3 Experiment on your calculator to find out what is missing on the blank keys. Write your answers.

a 1 · 4 + □ □ □ = 3.6

b □ □ □ + 2 · 5 = 9.8

c 1 · 8 + □ □ □ = 5.4

d □ □ □ + 6 · 4 = 10.

4 Investigate. Use these keys 2 3 4 5 as often as you like to go here:

□ · □ + □ · □ =

Make the calculator display as many different answers as you can. Record your additions.

Here is one way you might find.

2.3+4.5=6.8

STEPS 3b:23 57

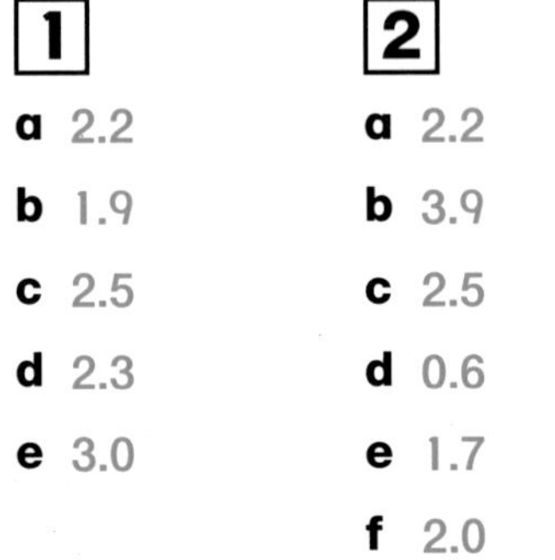
1

a 2.2
b 1.9
c 2.5
d 2.3
e 3.0

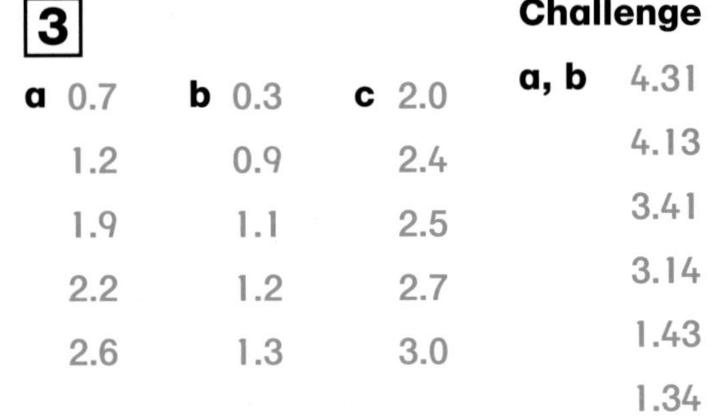
2

a 2.2
b 3.9
c 2.5
d 0.6
e 1.7
f 2.0

3

a	b	c
0.7	0.3	2.0
1.2	0.9	2.4
1.9	1.1	2.5
2.2	1.2	2.7
2.6	1.3	3.0

Challenge

a, b 4.31, 4.13, 3.41, 3.14, 1.43, 1.34

1

a 1.6	**b** 3.3	**c** 6.5
d 7.0	**e** 8.6	**f** 9.9
g 7.0	**h** 6.6	**i** 8.1

3

a 2.2 **b** 7.3 **c** 3.6 **d** 3.6

2

Open: finding at least 5 pairs of numbers which total 2.4.

4

Open: using keys 2, 3, 4, 5 to complete

□ · □ + □ · □ =

in as many ways as possible and record the results. (1/3 a,b,c)

BOOK 3b
PAGE 58

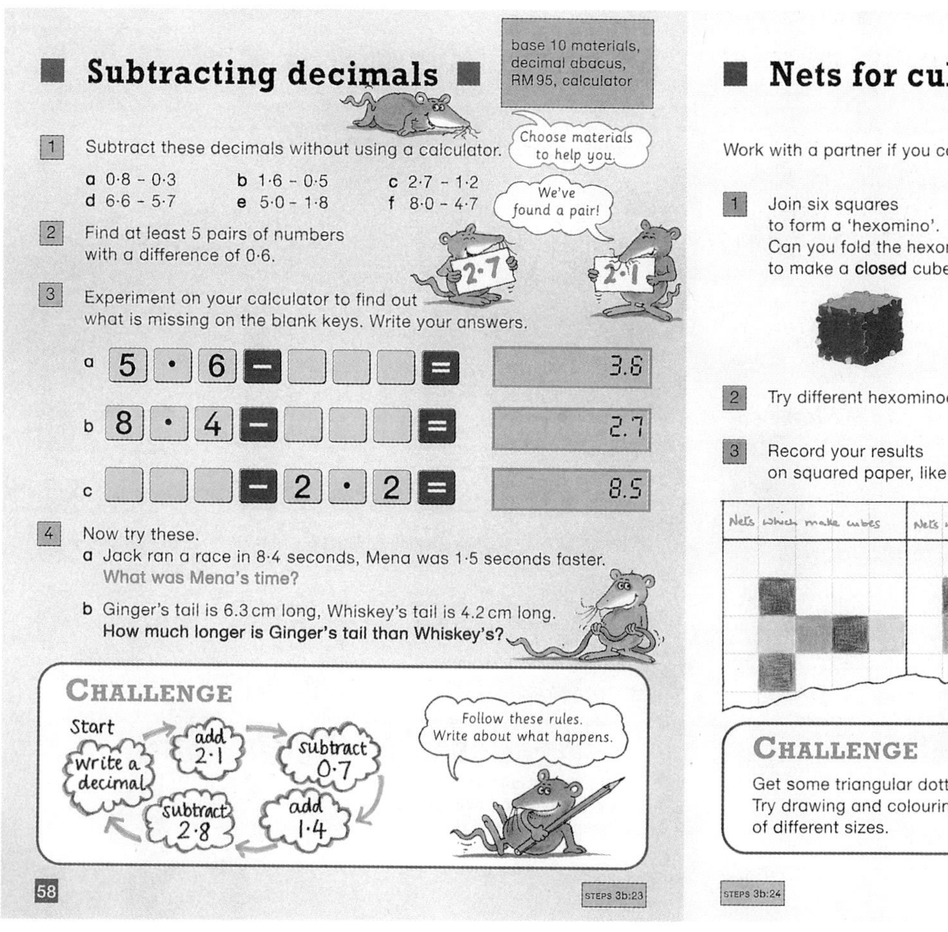

Subtracting decimals
base 10 materials, decimal abacus, RM95, calculator
1 Subtract these decimals without using a calculator.
a 0·8 – 0·3 b 1·6 – 0·5 c 2·7 – 1·2
d 6·6 – 5·7 e 5·0 – 1·8 f 8·0 – 4·7
Choose materials to help you.
We've found a pair!
2 Find at least 5 pairs of numbers with a difference of 0·6.
3 Experiment on your calculator to find out what is missing on the blank keys. Write your answers.
a 5 · 6 – = 3.6
b 8 · 4 – = 2.7
c – 2 · 2 = 8.5
4 Now try these.
a Jack ran a race in 8·4 seconds, Mena was 1·5 seconds faster. What was Mena's time?
b Ginger's tail is 6.3 cm long, Whiskey's tail is 4.2 cm long. How much longer is Ginger's tail than Whiskey's?
CHALLENGE
Start
write a decimal
add 2·1
subtract 0·7
add 1·4
subtract 2·8
Follow these rules. Write about what happens.
58
STEPS 3b:23

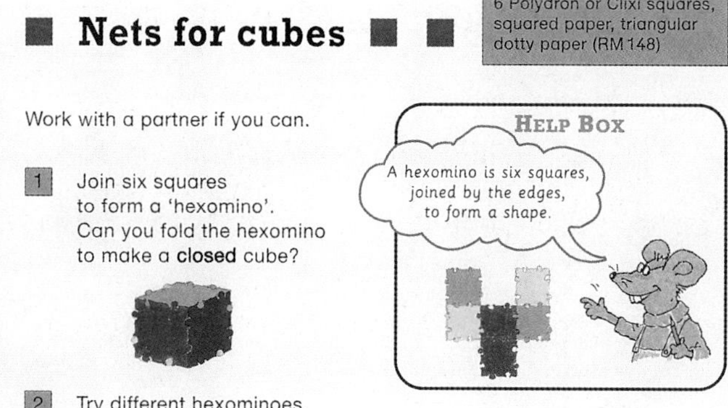

Nets for cubes
6 Polydron or Clixi squares, squared paper, triangular dotty paper (RM148)
Work with a partner if you can.
1 Join six squares to form a 'hexomino'. Can you fold the hexomino to make a closed cube?
HELP BOX
A hexomino is six squares, joined by the edges, to form a shape.
2 Try different hexominoes.
3 Record your results on squared paper, like this:
Will this fold to make a cube?
CHALLENGE
Get some triangular dotty paper. Try drawing and colouring cubes of different sizes.
STEPS 3b:24
59

BOOK 3b
PAGE 59

1 **2**

Practical: making closed cubes from hexominoes.

3

Recording hexominoes which make closed cubes. There are 35 possible hexominoes of which 11 do make closed cubes and 24 do not.

1

a 0.5 **b** 1.1

c 1.5 **d** 0.9

e 3.2 **f** 3.3

4

a 6.9 seconds

b 2.1 cm

2

Open: finding at least 5 pairs of numbers with a difference of 0.6.
(1/3 a,b,d)

Challenge

In each case the result should be the decimal started with.

3

a 2.0

b 5.7

c 10.7

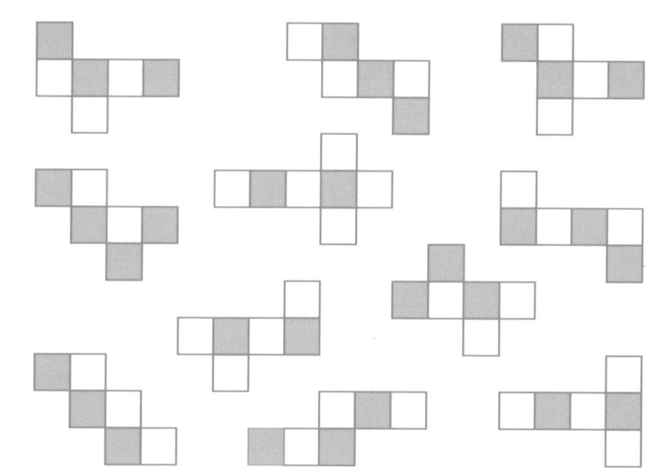

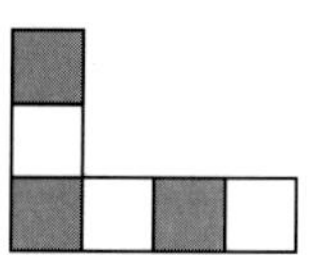

This hexomino does not make a closed cube.
(1/3 a,c)

Challenge

Drawing cubes of different sizes on triangular dotty paper.

BOOK 3b
PAGE 60

BOOK 3b
PAGE 61

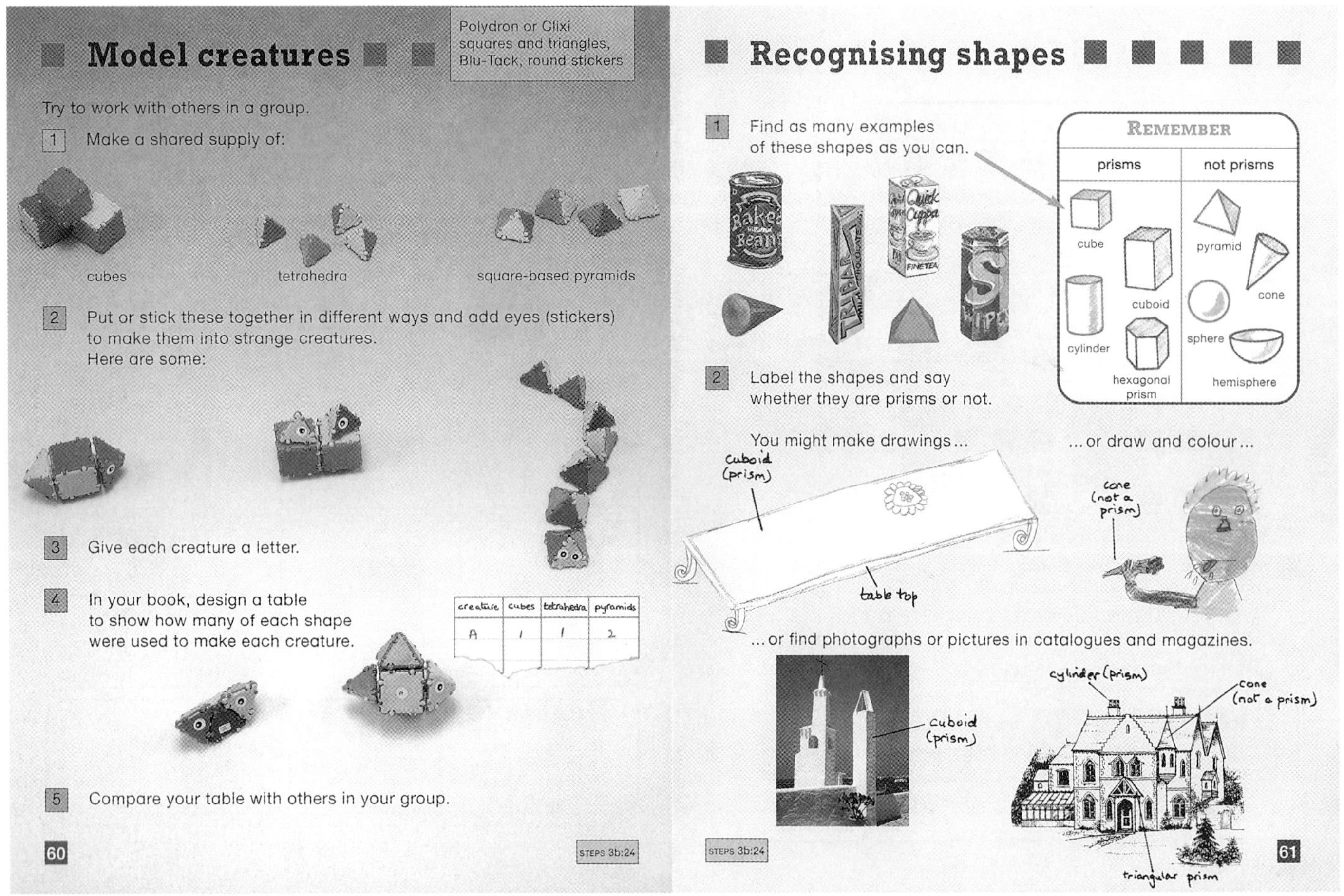

Model creatures

Polydron or Clixi squares and triangles, Blu-Tack, round stickers

Try to work with others in a group.

1 Make a shared supply of:

2 Put or stick these together in different ways and add eyes (stickers) to make them into strange creatures.
Here are some:

3 Give each creature a letter.

4 In your book, design a table to show how many of each shape were used to make each creature.

creature	cubes	tetrahedra	pyramids
A	1	1	2

5 Compare your table with others in your group.

60

STEPS 3b:24

Recognising shapes

1 Find as many examples of these shapes as you can.

REMEMBER

prisms	not prisms
cube, cuboid, cylinder, hexagonal prism	pyramid, cone, sphere, hemisphere

2 Label the shapes and say whether they are prisms or not.

You might make drawings …

… or draw and colour …

… or find photographs or pictures in catalogues and magazines.

STEPS 3b:24

61

Practical: making cubes, tetrahedra and square-based pyramids from Polydron or Clixi. Joining them to make strange creatures and recording how many of each shape are used. (1/3 b,c)

Practical: find examples of, and distinguish between, prisms and non-prisms.

BOOK 3b
PAGE 62

Order of adding

number cards

Use cards like these to help you if you need them.

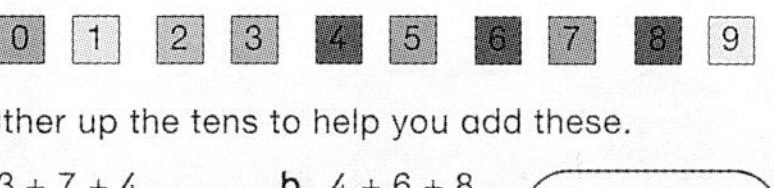

[1] Gather up the tens to help you add these.

a 3 + 7 + 4 b 4 + 6 + 8
c 8 + 8 + 2 d 9 + 1 + 9
e 5 + 7 + 3 f 10 + 0 + 7

[2] Make up six more examples like those in [1].

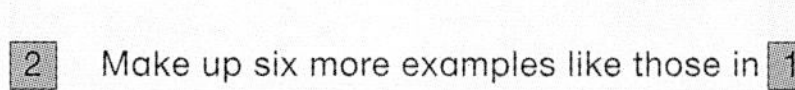

[3] Decide the easiest way to add these. Write down what you do.

a  b  c 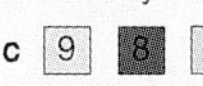

d e f 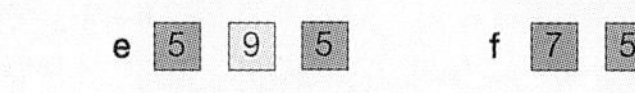

[4] Copy and complete these pairs. Put a loop round the way you find easier in each pair.

a (9 + 1) + 7 = b (8 + 5) + 5 = c (7 + 3) + 8 =
9 + (1 + 7) = 8 + (5 + 5) = 7 + (3 + 8) =

Make at least six more sums like this. The answer must be 20 each time

CHALLENGE

(4 + 6) + (7 + 3) = 20

62 STEPS 3b:25

1

a (3 + 7) + 4 = 14
b (4 + 6) + 8 = 18
c 8 + (8 + 2) = 18
d (9 + 1) + 9 = 19
e 5 + (7 + 3) = 15
f 10 + 0 + 7 = 17

2

Open: making up six more examples like those in 1. (1/3 a)

3

a (3 + 7) + 8 = 18
b (4 + 6) + 8 = 18
c (9 + 1) + 8 = 18
d (6 + 4) + 7 = 17
e (5 + 5) + 9 = 19
f (7 + 3) + 5 = 15

4

a (9 + 1) + 7 = 17
9 + (7 + 1) = 17
b (8 + 5) + 5 = 18
8 + (5 + 5) = 18
c (7 + 3) + 8 = 18
7 + (3 + 8) = 18

Challenge

Open: making up at least 6 more sums in which 4 numbers are paired off to make 2 tens and and a total of 20. (1/3 b,d)

BOOK 3b
PAGE 63

> and <

[1] Copy and complete these.

a 8 + 5 = b 9 + 4 =
c 7 + 6 = d 7 + 9 =
e 11 + 7 = f 14 + 5 =
g 17 + 3 = h 13 + 6 =

Use the answers to help you with the rest of the page.

REMEMBER

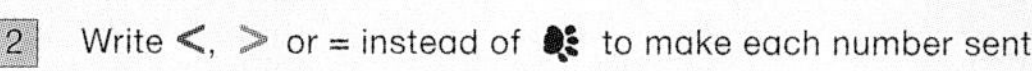

[2] Write <, > or = instead of 🐾 to make each number sentence true.

a 8 + 5 🐾 7 + 9 b 11 + 7 🐾 8 + 5 c 7 + 6 🐾 9 + 4
d 13 + 6 🐾 14 + 5 e 17 + 3 🐾 11 + 7 f 11 + 7 🐾 7 + 6
g 9 + 4 🐾 13 + 6 h 14 + 5 🐾 17 + 3 i 8 + 5 🐾 9 + 4

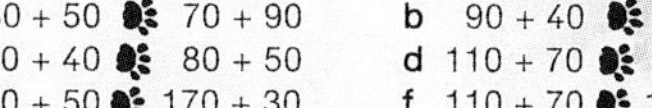

[3] Do these in the same way as [2].

a 80 + 50 🐾 70 + 90 b 90 + 40 🐾 70 + 60
c 90 + 40 🐾 80 + 50 d 110 + 70 🐾 70 + 90
e 80 + 50 🐾 170 + 30 f 110 + 70 🐾 140 + 50

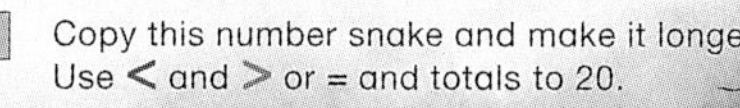

[4] Copy this number snake and make it longer. Use < and > or = and totals to 20.

STEPS 3b:25 63

1

a 8 + 5 = 13
b 9 + 4 = 13
c 7 + 6 = 13
d 7 + 9 = 16
e 11 + 7 = 18
f 14 + 5 = 19
g 17 + 3 = 20
h 13 + 6 = 19

2

a 8 + 5 < 7 + 9
b 11 + 7 > 8 + 5
c 7 + 6 = 9 + 4
d 13 + 6 = 14 + 5
e 17 + 3 > 11 + 7
f 11 + 7 > 7 + 6
g 9 + 4 < 13 + 6
h 14 + 5 < 17 + 3
i 8 + 5 = 9 + 4

3

a 80 + 60 < 70 + 90
b 90 + 40 = 70 + 60
c 90 + 40 = 80 + 50
d 110 + 70 < 70 + 90
e 80 + 50 < 170 + 30
f 110 + 70 < 140 + 50

4

Open: copying and completing a chain of additions separated by <, = or >.

BOOK 3b
PAGE 64

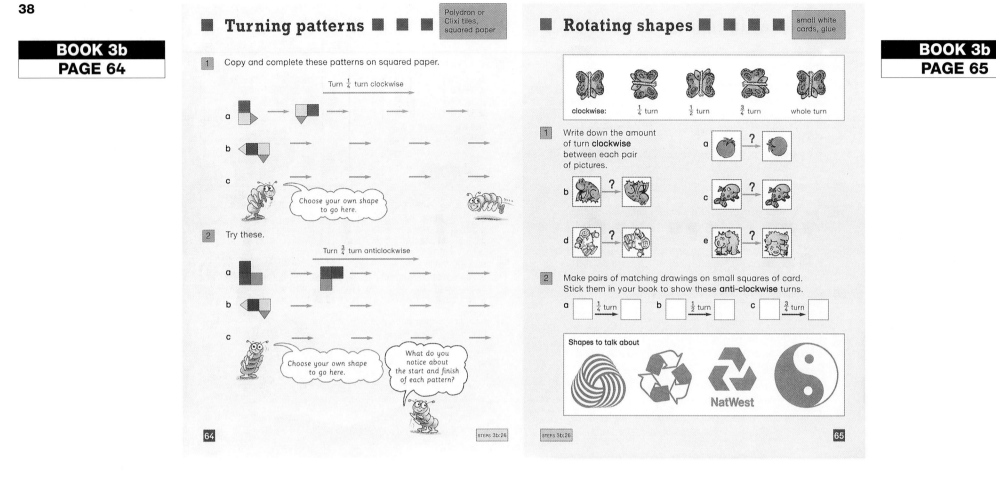

Turning patterns

Polydron or Clixi tiles, squared paper

1 Copy and complete these patterns on squared paper.

Turn $\frac{1}{4}$ turn clockwise

a

b

c

Choose your own shape to go here.

2 Try these.

Turn $\frac{3}{4}$ turn anticlockwise

a

b

c

Choose your own shape to go here.

What do you notice about the start and finish of each pattern?

BOOK 3b
PAGE 65

Rotating shapes

small white cards, glue

clockwise: $\frac{1}{4}$ turn $\frac{1}{2}$ turn $\frac{3}{4}$ turn whole turn

1 Write down the amount of turn **clockwise** between each pair of pictures.

a ?

b ?

c ?

d ?

e ?

2 Make pairs of matching drawings on small squares of card. Stick them in your book to show these **anti-clockwise** turns.

a $\frac{1}{4}$ turn b $\frac{1}{2}$ turn c $\frac{3}{4}$ turn

Shapes to talk about

NatWest

1

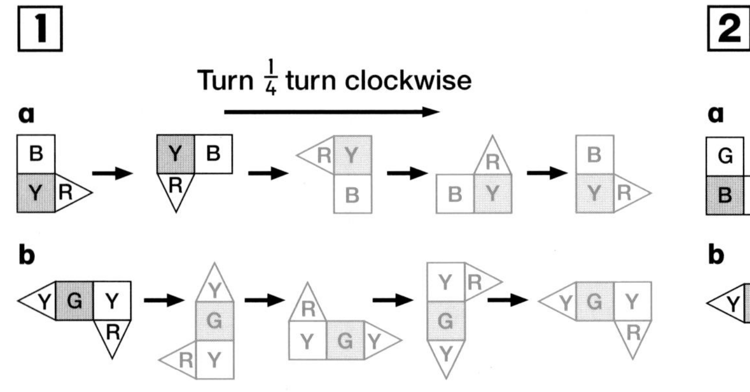

c Open: choose own shapes to rotate. (1/3 c)

2

Turn $\frac{3}{4}$ turn anticlockwise

a

G B R → B G R → R B G → R G B → G B R

b

Y G Y R → Y G R Y → R Y G Y → Y R G Y → Y G Y R

c Open: choose own shapes to rotate. (1/3 c)

1

a $\frac{3}{4}$ turn
b $\frac{1}{2}$ turn
c whole turn
d $\frac{1}{4}$ turn
e $\frac{3}{4}$ turn

2

Practical: making pairs of matching drawings on small square to show:

a $\frac{1}{4}$ anti-clockwise
b $\frac{1}{2}$ turn anti-clockwise
c $\frac{3}{4}$ turn anti-clockwise.

(1/3 a,b)

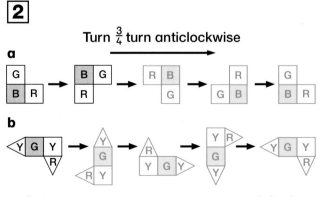

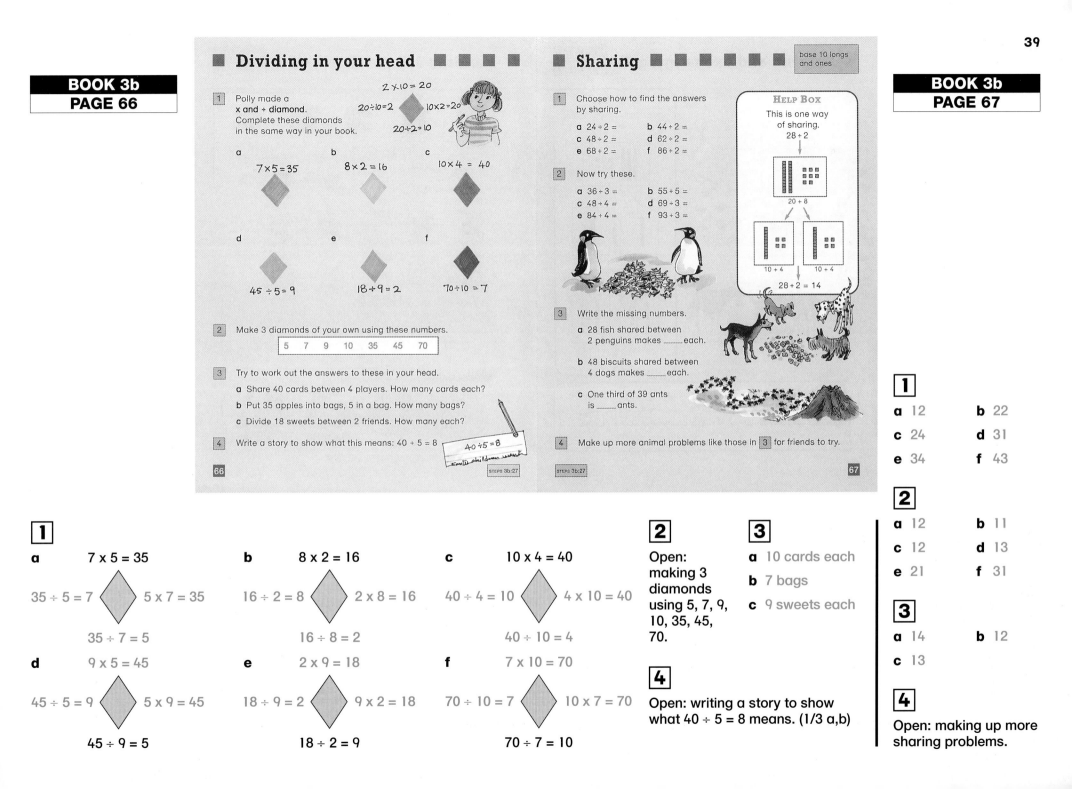

BOOK 3b
PAGE 66

Dividing in your head

1 Polly made a **x and ÷ diamond**. Complete these diamonds in the same way in your book.

2 x 10 = 20, 10 x 2 = 20, 20 ÷ 2 = 10, 20 ÷ 10 = 2

a 7 x 5 = 35

b 8 x 2 = 16

c 10 x 4 = 40

d 45 ÷ 5 = 9

e 18 ÷ 9 = 2

f 70 ÷ 10 = 7

2 Make 3 diamonds of your own using these numbers.

5	7	9	10	35	45	70

3 Try to work out the answers to these in your head.

a Share 40 cards between 4 players. How many cards each?

b Put 35 apples into bags, 5 in a bag. How many bags?

c Divide 18 sweets between 2 friends. How many each?

4 Write a story to show what this means: 40 ÷ 5 = 8

66 STEPS 3b:27

Sharing

base 10 longs and ones

1 Choose how to find the answers by sharing.

a 24 ÷ 2 = b 44 ÷ 2 =
c 48 ÷ 2 = d 62 ÷ 2 =
e 68 ÷ 2 = f 86 ÷ 2 =

Help Box
This is one way of sharing.
28 ÷ 2
20 + 8
10 + 4 10 + 4
28 ÷ 2 = 14

2 Now try these.

a 36 ÷ 3 = b 55 ÷ 5 =
c 48 ÷ 4 = d 69 ÷ 3 =
e 84 ÷ 4 = f 93 ÷ 3 =

3 Write the missing numbers.

a 28 fish shared between 2 penguins makes ____ each.

b 48 biscuits shared between 4 dogs makes ____ each.

c One third of 39 ants is ____ ants.

4 Make up more animal problems like those in 3 for friends to try.

STEPS 3b:27 67

BOOK 3b
PAGE 67

1

a 12 b 22
c 24 d 31
e 34 f 43

2

a 12 b 11
c 12 d 13
e 21 f 31

3

a 14 b 12
c 13

4

Open: making up more sharing problems.

1

a 7 x 5 = 35

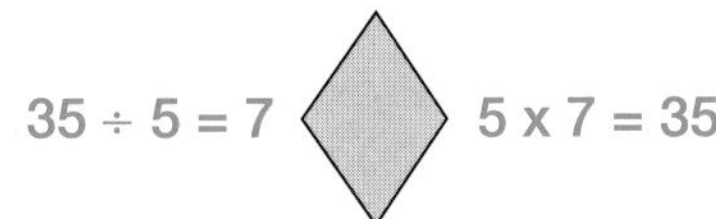

b 8 x 2 = 16

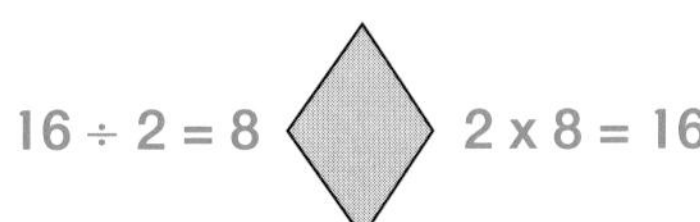

c 10 x 4 = 40

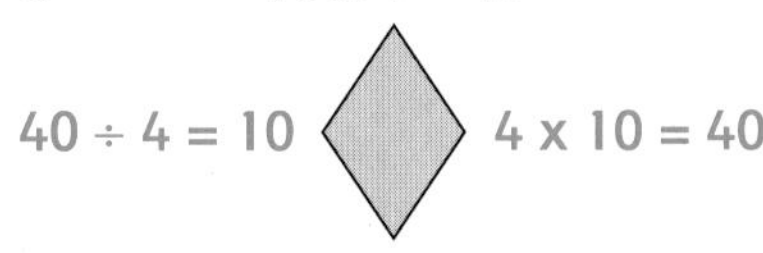

d 9 x 5 = 45

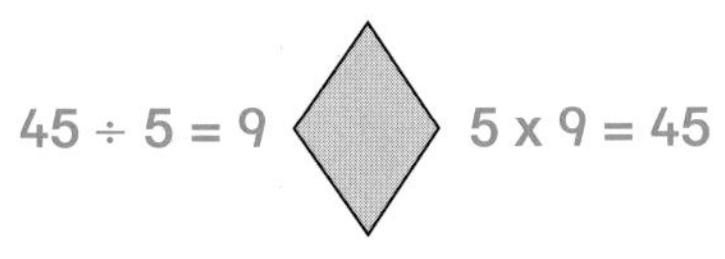

e 2 x 9 = 18

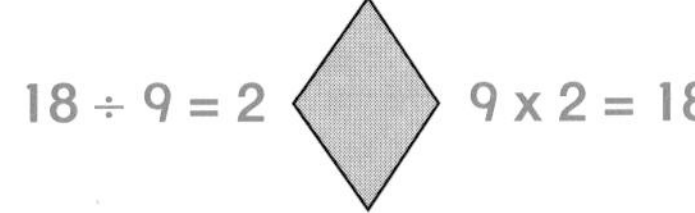

f 7 x 10 = 70

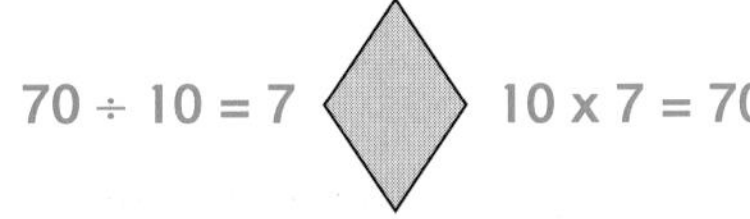

2

Open: making 3 diamonds using 5, 7, 9, 10, 35, 45, 70.

3

a 10 cards each
b 7 bags
c 9 sweets each

4

Open: writing a story to show what 40 ÷ 5 = 8 means. (1/3 a,b)

BOOK 3b
PAGE 68

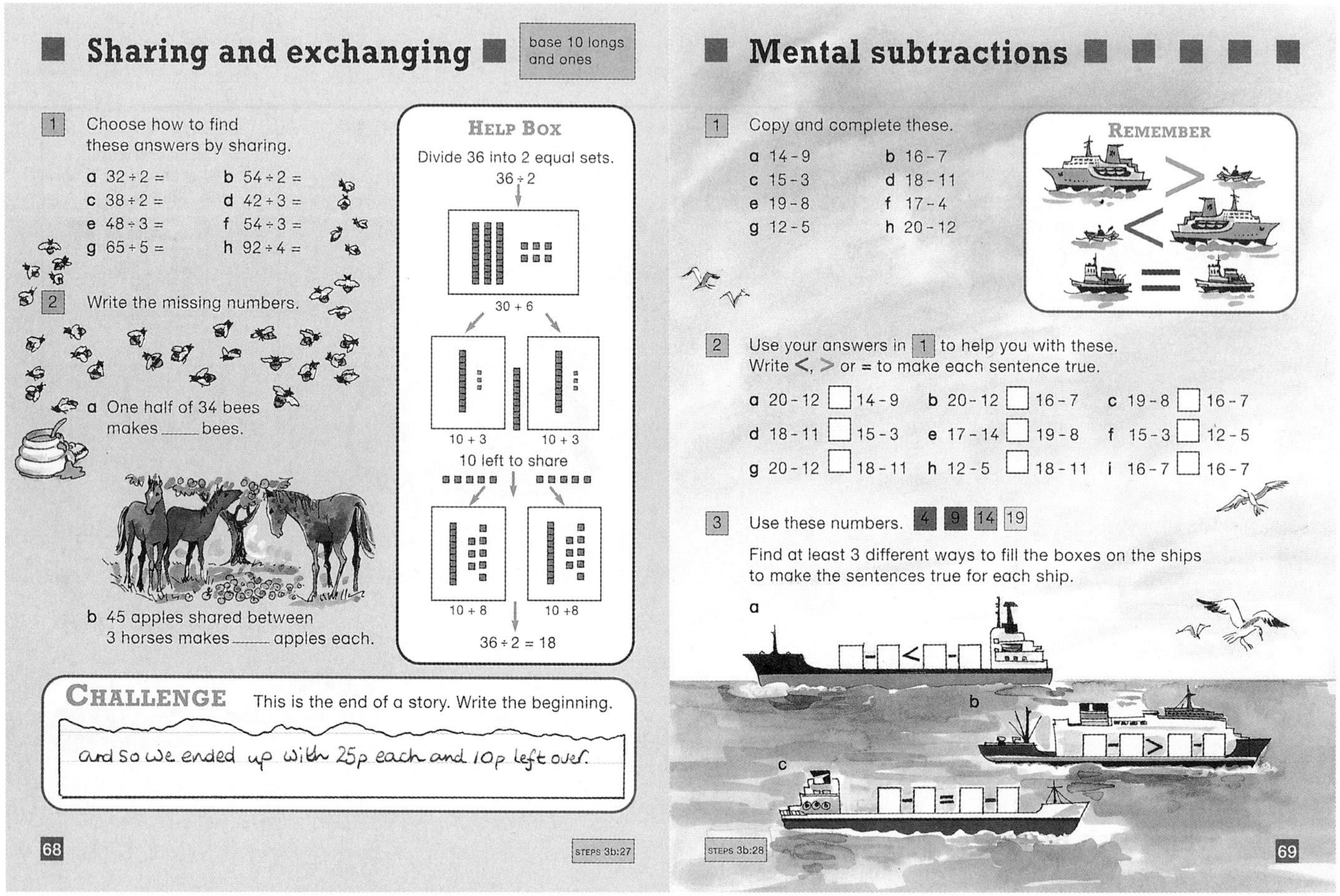

Sharing and exchanging

base 10 longs and ones

1 Choose how to find these answers by sharing.

a 32 ÷ 2 = b 54 ÷ 2 =
c 38 ÷ 2 = d 42 ÷ 3 =
e 48 ÷ 3 = f 54 ÷ 3 =
g 65 ÷ 5 = h 92 ÷ 4 =

2 Write the missing numbers.

a One half of 34 bees makes ____ bees.

b 45 apples shared between 3 horses makes ____ apples each.

HELP BOX

Divide 36 into 2 equal sets.

36 ÷ 2

30 + 6

10 + 3 10 + 3

10 left to share

10 + 8 10 + 8

36 ÷ 2 = 18

CHALLENGE This is the end of a story. Write the beginning.

and so we ended up with 25p each and 10p left over.

BOOK 3b
PAGE 69

Mental subtractions

1 Copy and complete these.

a 14 - 9 b 16 - 7
c 15 - 3 d 18 - 11
e 19 - 8 f 17 - 4
g 12 - 5 h 20 - 12

REMEMBER

> < =

2 Use your answers in 1 to help you with these.
Write <, > or = to make each sentence true.

a 20 - 12 ☐ 14 - 9 b 20 - 12 ☐ 16 - 7 c 19 - 8 ☐ 16 - 7
d 18 - 11 ☐ 15 - 3 e 17 - 14 ☐ 19 - 8 f 15 - 3 ☐ 12 - 5
g 20 - 12 ☐ 18 - 11 h 12 - 5 ☐ 18 - 11 i 16 - 7 ☐ 16 - 7

3 Use these numbers. 4 9 14 19

Find at least 3 different ways to fill the boxes on the ships to make the sentences true for each ship.

a ☐ - ☐ < ☐ - ☐

b ☐ - ☐ > ☐ - ☐

c ☐ - ☐ = ☐ - ☐

1

a 16
b 27
c 19
d 14
e 16
f 18
g 13
h 23

2

a 17
b 15

3

Challenge

Write a story ending: *and so we ended up with 25p each and 10p left over.*
(1/3 a,b)

1

a 14 – 9 = 5
b 16 – 7 = 9
c 15 – 3 = 12
d 18 – 11 = 7
e 19 – 8 = 11
f 17 – 4 = 13
g 12 – 5 = 7
h 20 – 12 = 8

2

a 20 – 12 > 14 – 9
b 20 – 12 < 16 – 7
c 19 – 8 > 16 – 7
d 18 – 11 < 15 – 3
e 17 – 14 < 19 – 8
f 15 – 3 > 12 – 5
g 20 – 12 > 18 – 11
h 12 – 5 = 18 – 11
i 16 – 7 = 16 – 7

3

Open: using the numbers 4, 9, 14, 19 to make different true subtraction sentences containing <, > and =.

BOOK 3b
PAGE 70

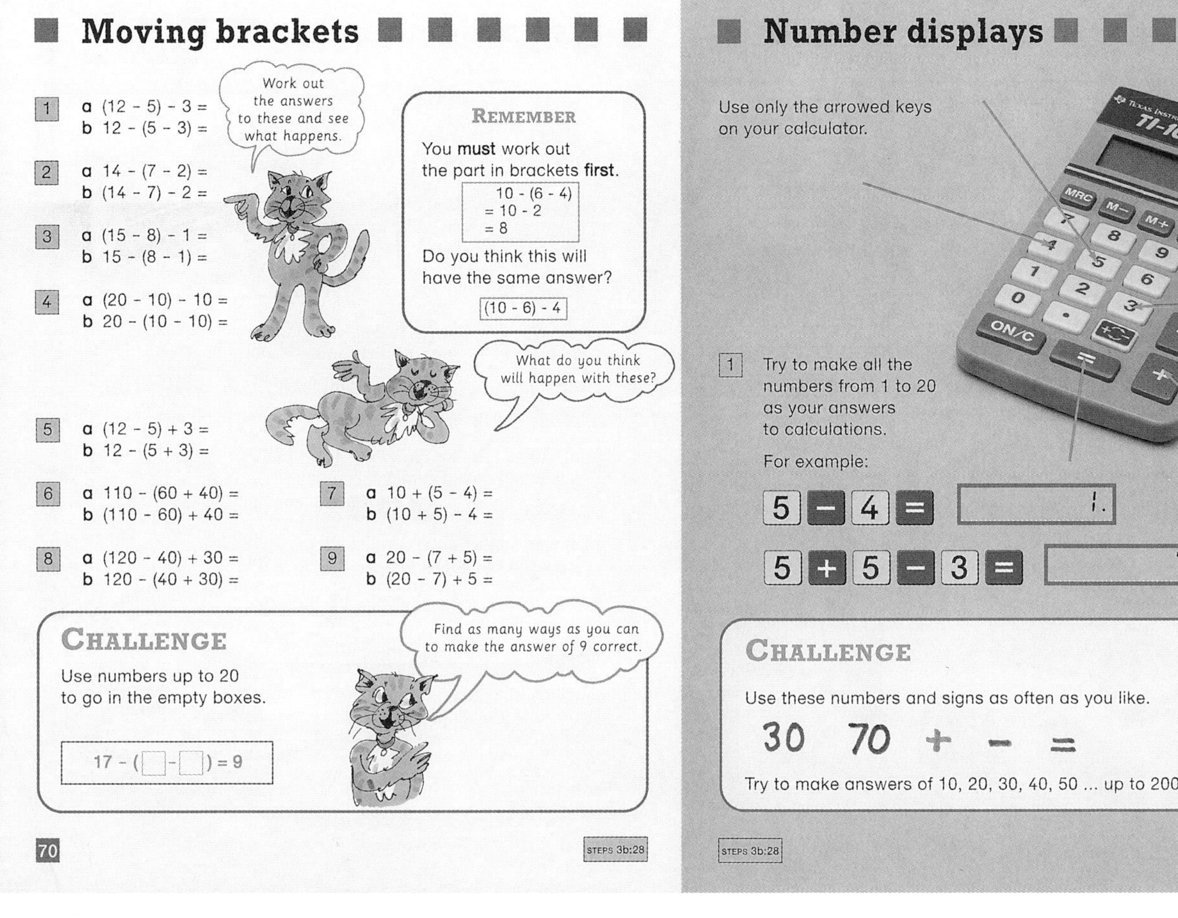

BOOK 3b
PAGE 71

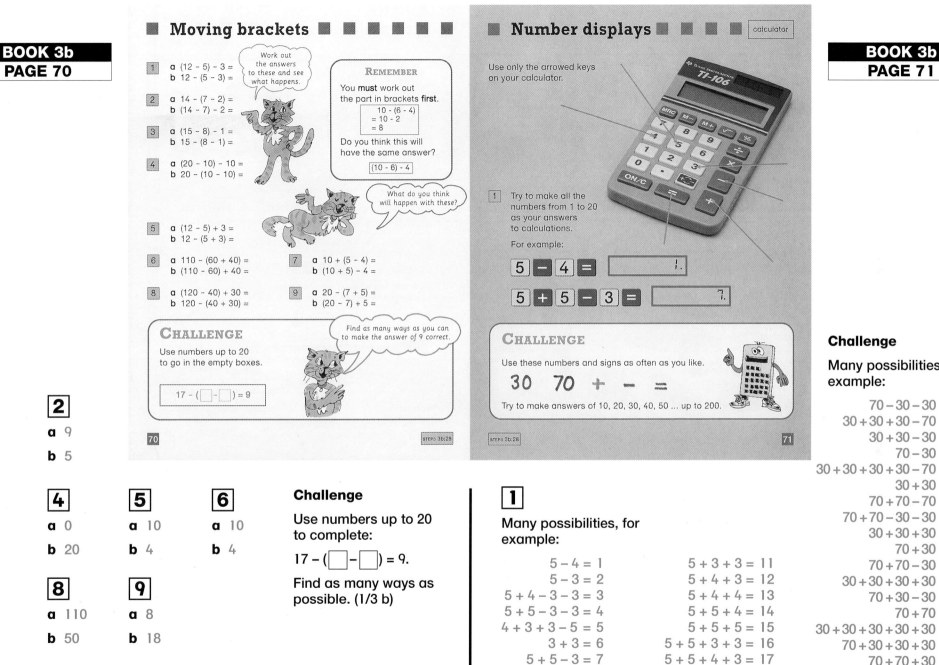

1
a 4
b 10

2
a 9
b 5

3
a 6
b 8

4
a 0
b 20

5
a 10
b 4

6
a 10
b 4

7
a 11
b 11

8
a 110
b 50

9
a 8
b 18

Challenge

Use numbers up to 20 to complete:

17 – (☐ – ☐) = 9.

Find as many ways as possible. (1/3 b)

1

Many possibilities, for example:

5 – 4 = 1
5 – 3 = 2
5 + 4 – 3 – 3 = 3
5 + 5 – 3 – 3 = 4
4 + 3 + 3 – 5 = 5
3 + 3 = 6
5 + 5 – 3 = 7
4 + 4 = 8
5 + 4 = 9
5 + 5 = 10
5 + 3 + 3 = 11
5 + 4 + 3 = 12
5 + 4 + 4 = 13
5 + 5 + 4 = 14
5 + 5 + 5 = 15
5 + 5 + 3 + 3 = 16
5 + 5 + 4 + 3 = 17
5 + 5 + 4 + 4 = 18
5 + 5 + 5 + 4 = 19
5 + 5 + 5 + 5 = 20

Challenge

Many possibilities, for example:

70 – 30 – 30 = 10
30 + 30 + 30 – 70 = 20
30 + 30 – 30 = 30
70 – 30 = 40
30 + 30 + 30 + 30 – 70 = 50
30 + 30 = 60
70 + 70 – 70 = 70
70 + 70 – 30 – 30 = 80
30 + 30 + 30 = 90
70 + 30 = 100
70 + 70 – 30 = 110
30 + 30 + 30 + 30 = 120
70 + 30 – 30 = 130
70 + 70 = 140
30 + 30 + 30 + 30 + 30 = 150
70 + 30 + 30 + 30 = 160
70 + 70 + 30 = 170
70 + 70 + 70 – 30 = 180
70 + 30 + 30 + 30 + 30 = 190
70 + 70 + 30 + 30 = 200

BOOK 3b
PAGE 72

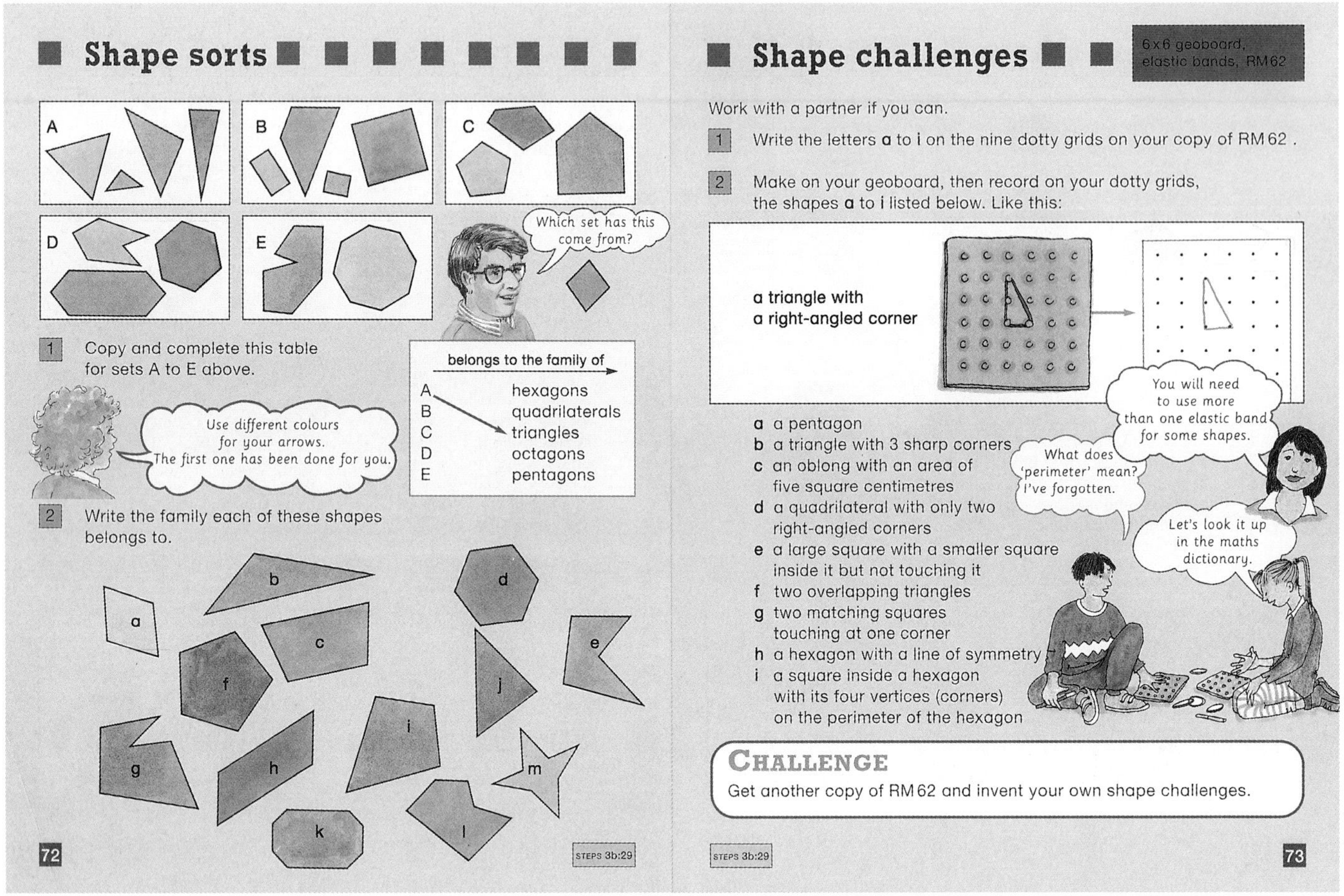

Shape sorts

A B C D E

Which set has this come from?

1 Copy and complete this table for sets A to E above.

Use different colours for your arrows. The first one has been done for you.

	belongs to the family of
A	hexagons
B	quadrilaterals
C	triangles
D	octagons
E	pentagons

2 Write the family each of these shapes belongs to.

a b c d e f g h i j k l m

72 STEPS 3b:29

Shape challenges

6x6 geoboard, elastic bands, RM 62

Work with a partner if you can.

1 Write the letters **a** to **i** on the nine dotty grids on your copy of RM 62 .

2 Make on your geoboard, then record on your dotty grids, the shapes **a** to **i** listed below. Like this:

a triangle with a right-angled corner

- **a** a pentagon
- **b** a triangle with 3 sharp corners
- **c** an oblong with an area of five square centimetres
- **d** a quadrilateral with only two right-angled corners
- **e** a large square with a smaller square inside it but not touching it
- **f** two overlapping triangles
- **g** two matching squares touching at one corner
- **h** a hexagon with a line of symmetry
- **i** a square inside a hexagon with its four vertices (corners) on the perimeter of the hexagon

You will need to use more than one elastic band for some shapes.

What does 'perimeter' mean? I've forgotten.

Let's look it up in the maths dictionary.

CHALLENGE
Get another copy of RM 62 and invent your own shape challenges.

STEPS 3b:29 73

BOOK 3b
PAGE 73

1 **2**

Some possible solutions:

a

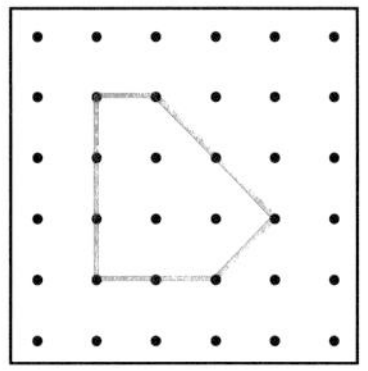

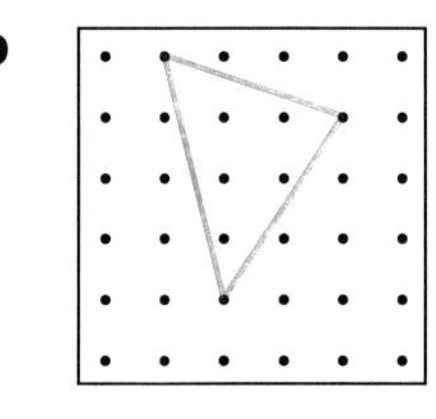

b

1

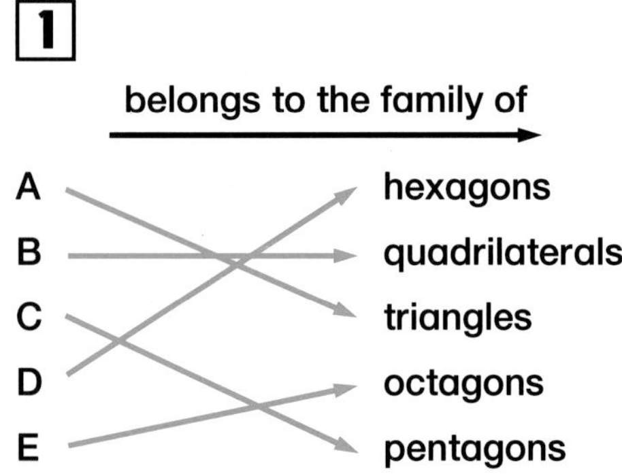

2

triangles: **b, j**

quadrilaterals: **a, c, h, i**

pentagons: **e, f**

hexagons: **d, g, l**

octagons: **k, m**

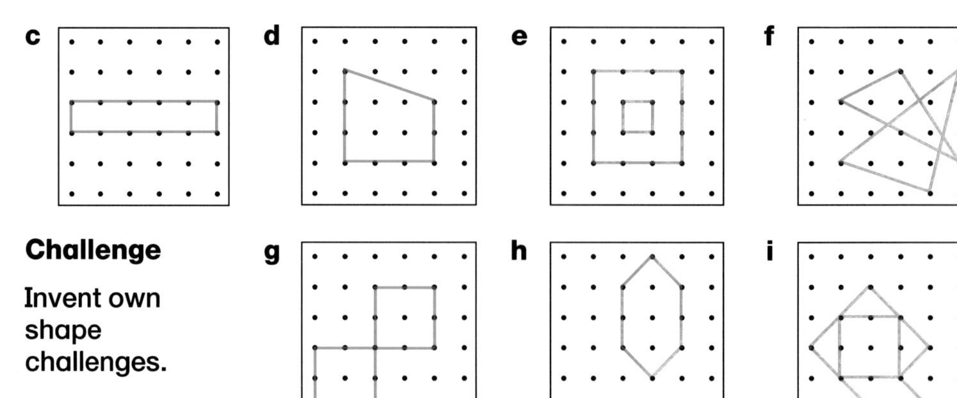

Challenge

Invent own shape challenges.

BOOK 3b
PAGE 74

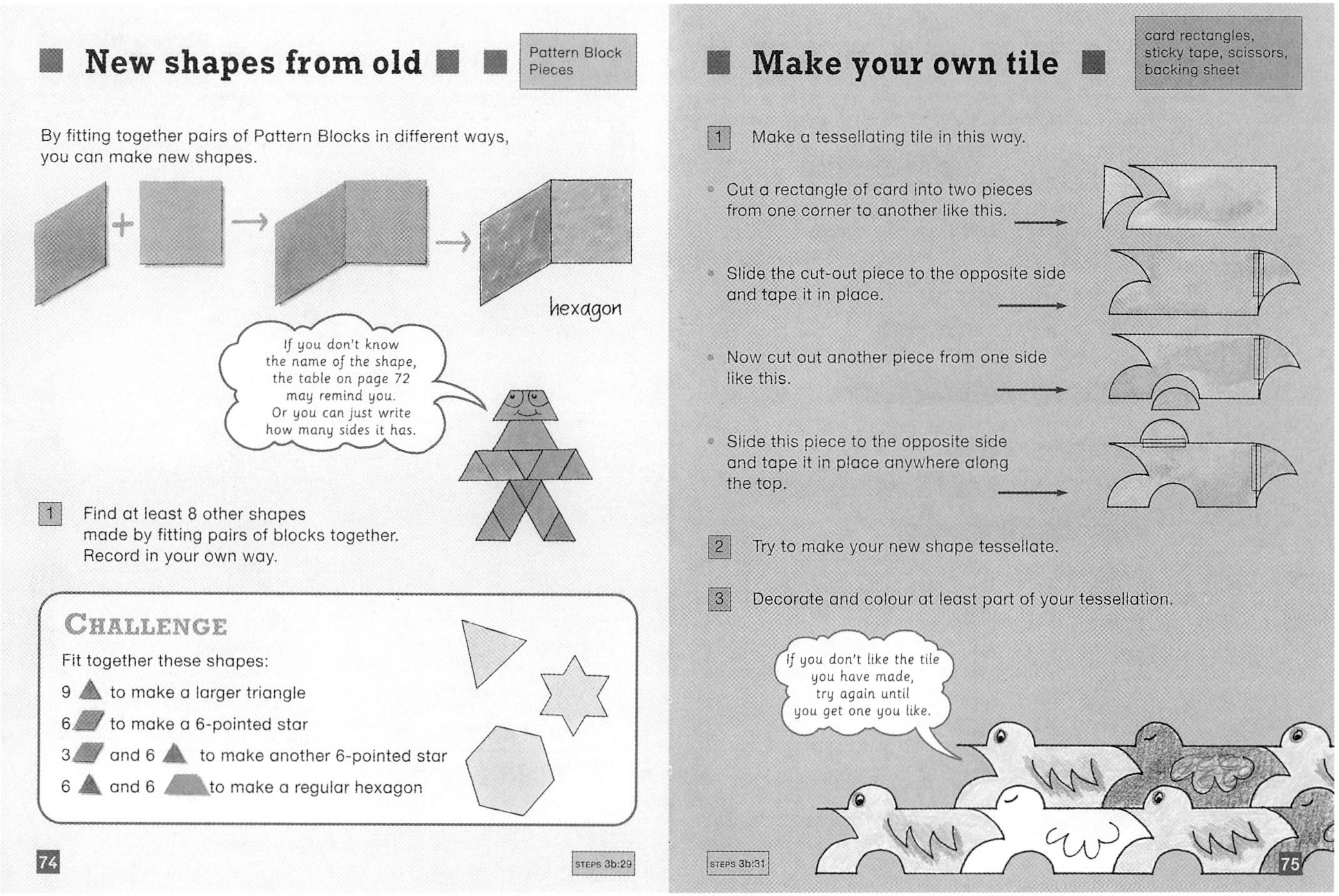

New shapes from old

Pattern Block Pieces

By fitting together pairs of Pattern Blocks in different ways, you can make new shapes.

hexagon

If you don't know the name of the shape, the table on page 72 may remind you. Or you can just write how many sides it has.

1 Find at least 8 other shapes made by fitting pairs of blocks together. Record in your own way.

Challenge

Fit together these shapes:

9 ▲ to make a larger triangle

6 ▱ to make a 6-pointed star

3 ▱ and 6 ▲ to make another 6-pointed star

6 ▲ and 6 ⏢ to make a regular hexagon

74 STEPS 3b:29

BOOK 3b
PAGE 75

Make your own tile

card rectangles, sticky tape, scissors, backing sheet

1 Make a tessellating tile in this way.

- Cut a rectangle of card into two pieces from one corner to another like this.
- Slide the cut-out piece to the opposite side and tape it in place.
- Now cut out another piece from one side like this.
- Slide this piece to the opposite side and tape it in place anywhere along the top.

2 Try to make your new shape tessellate.

3 Decorate and colour at least part of your tessellation.

If you don't like the tile you have made, try again until you get one you like.

STEPS 3b:31 75

1

Practical: finding at least 6 other shapes by fitting pairs of blocks together.

Challenge

Some possible solutions: (1/3 a)

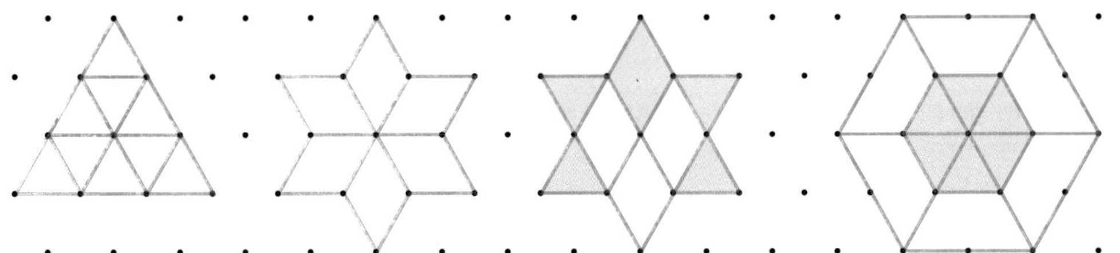

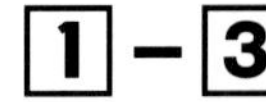

Practical: creating tessellating tiles.

BOOK 3b
PAGE 76

Using scale

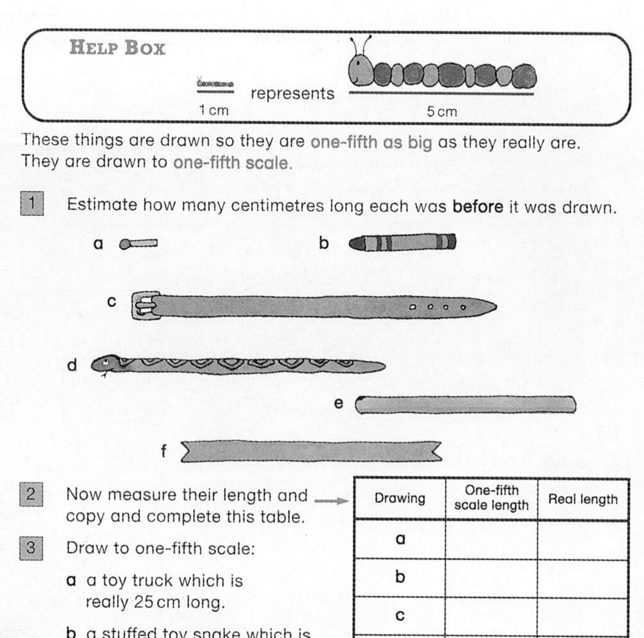

HELP BOX

1 cm represents 5 cm

These things are drawn so they are one-fifth as big as they really are. They are drawn to one-fifth scale.

1 Estimate how many centimetres long each was **before** it was drawn.

a b c d e f

2 Now measure their length and copy and complete this table.

Drawing	One-fifth scale length	Real length
a		
b		
c		
d		
e		
f		

3 Draw to one-fifth scale:

a a toy truck which is really 25 cm long.

b a stuffed toy snake which is really 40 cm long.

76 STEPS 3b:32

BOOK 3b
PAGE 77

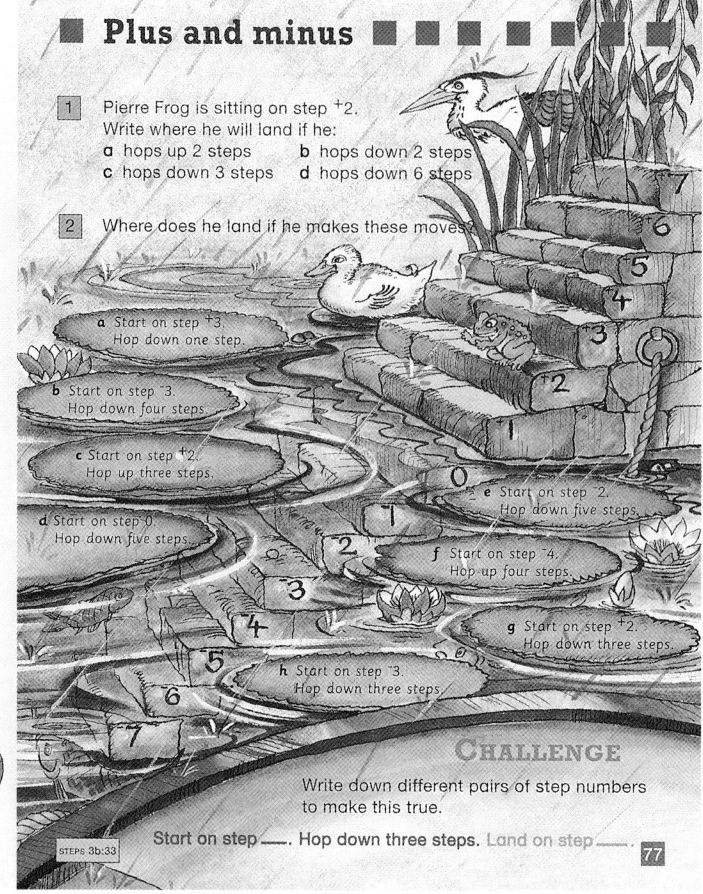

Plus and minus

1 Pierre Frog is sitting on step $^{+}2$.
Write where he will land if he:
a hops up 2 steps b hops down 2 steps
c hops down 3 steps d hops down 6 steps

2 Where does he land if he makes these moves?

a Start on step $^{+}3$. Hop down one step.
b Start on step $^{-}3$. Hop down four steps.
c Start on step $^{+}2$. Hop up three steps.
d Start on step 0. Hop down five steps.
e Start on step $^{-}2$. Hop down five steps.
f Start on step $^{-}4$. Hop up four steps.
g Start on step $^{+}2$. Hop down three steps.
h Start on step $^{-}3$. Hop down three steps.

CHALLENGE

Write down different pairs of step numbers to make this true.

Start on step ___. Hop down three steps. Land on step ___.

STEPS 3b:33 77

1

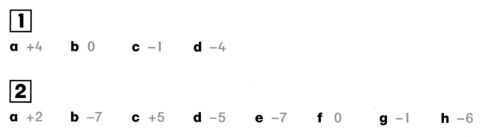

Estimating lengths of real objects from scale drawings. Reasonable estimates would be within about 5cm of:

a 5cm **b** 15cm
c 50cm **d** 40cm
e 30cm **f** 35cm

2

Drawing	1/5 scale length	Real length
a	1cm	5cm
b	3cm	15cm
c	10cm	50cm
d	8cm	40cm
e	6cm	30cm
f	7cm	35cm

3

Practical: drawing to one-fifth scale.

1

a +4 **b** 0 **c** −1 **d** −4

2

a +2 **b** −7 **c** +5 **d** −5 **e** −7 **f** 0 **g** −1 **h** −6

Challenge

Writing down different pairs of step numbers for:
Start on step ___ . Hop down three steps. Land on step ___ . (1/3 b)

BOOK 3b
PAGE 78

Temperatures

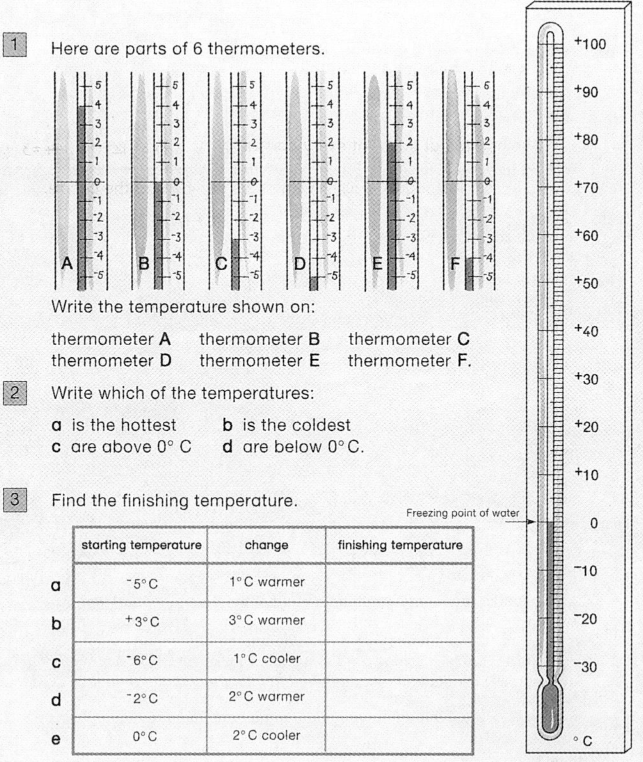

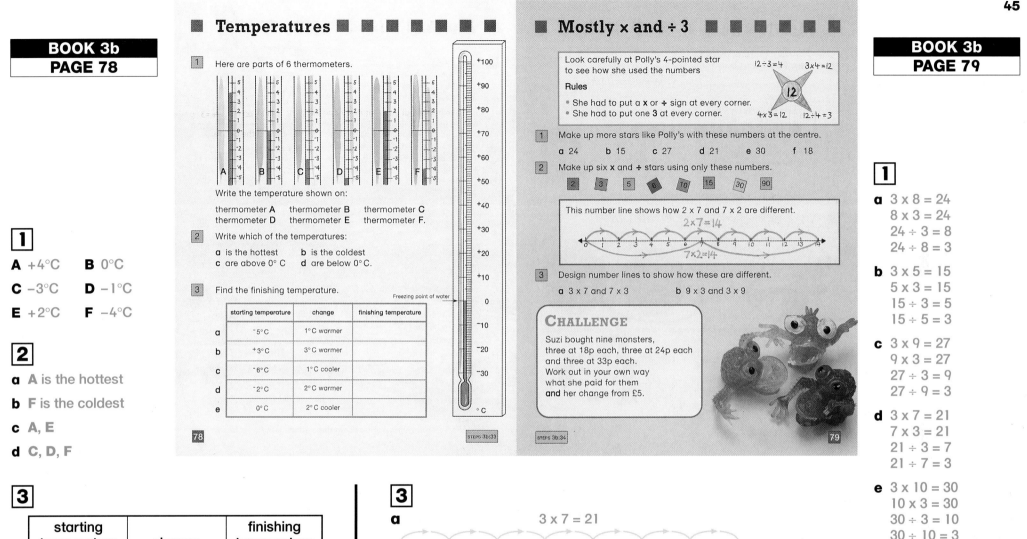

1 Here are parts of 6 thermometers.

Write the temperature shown on:

thermometer A thermometer B thermometer C
thermometer D thermometer E thermometer F.

2 Write which of the temperatures:

a is the hottest b is the coldest
c are above 0° C d are below 0° C.

3 Find the finishing temperature.

	starting temperature	change	finishing temperature
a	⁻5°C	1°C warmer	
b	⁺3°C	3°C warmer	
c	⁻6°C	1°C cooler	
d	⁻2°C	2°C warmer	
e	0°C	2°C cooler	

78 STEPS 3b:33

1

A +4°C **B** 0°C
C −3°C **D** −1°C
E +2°C **F** −4°C

2

a A is the hottest
b F is the coldest
c A, E
d C, D, F

3

	starting temperature	change	finishing temperature
a	−5°C	1°C warmer	−4°C
b	+3°C	3°C warmer	+6°C
c	−6°C	1°C cooler	−7°C
d	−2°C	2°C warmer	0°C
e	0°C	2°C cooler	−2°C

BOOK 3b
PAGE 79

Mostly x and ÷ 3

Look carefully at Polly's 4-pointed star to see how she used the numbers

Rules
- She had to put a **x** or **÷** sign at every corner.
- She had to put one **3** at every corner.

1 Make up more stars like Polly's with these numbers at the centre.

a 24 b 15 c 27 d 21 e 30 f 18

2 Make up six **x** and **÷** stars using only these numbers.

2 3 5 6 10 15 30 90

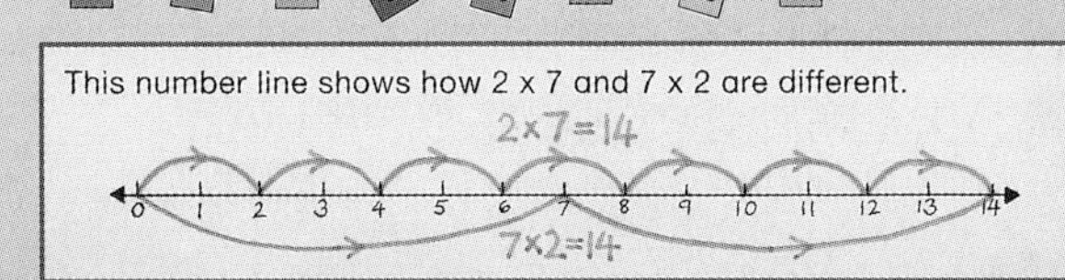

This number line shows how 2 x 7 and 7 x 2 are different.

3 Design number lines to show how these are different.

a 3 x 7 and 7 x 3 b 9 x 3 and 3 x 9

CHALLENGE

Suzi bought nine monsters, three at 18p each, three at 24p each and three at 33p each.
Work out in your own way what she paid for them and her change from £5.

STEPS 3b:34 79

1

a 3 x 8 = 24
8 x 3 = 24
24 ÷ 3 = 8
24 ÷ 8 = 3

b 3 x 5 = 15
5 x 3 = 15
15 ÷ 3 = 5
15 ÷ 5 = 3

c 3 x 9 = 27
9 x 3 = 27
27 ÷ 3 = 9
27 ÷ 9 = 3

d 3 x 7 = 21
7 x 3 = 21
21 ÷ 3 = 7
21 ÷ 7 = 3

e 3 x 10 = 30
10 x 3 = 30
30 ÷ 3 = 10
30 ÷ 10 = 3

f 3 x 6 = 18
6 x 3 = 18
18 ÷ 3 = 6
18 ÷ 6 = 3

2

Open: making up six stars using only 2, 3, 5, 6, 10, 15, 30, 90.

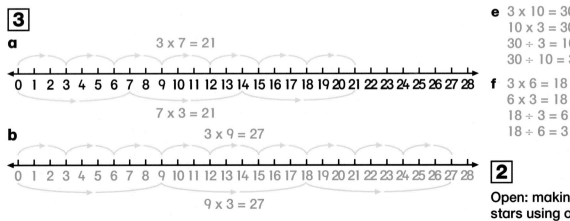

3

a

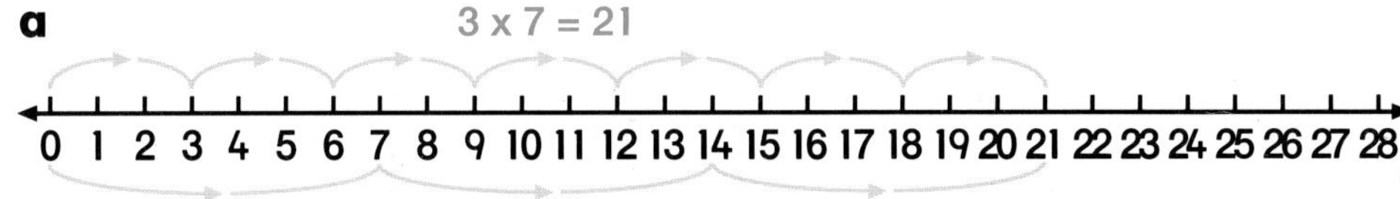

b

Challenge Total cost: £2.25; change from £5: £2.75 **(1/3 a,b)**

BOOK 3b PAGE 80

Mostly x and ÷ 4

1 Make five more 4-pointed stars like Polly's on page 79.

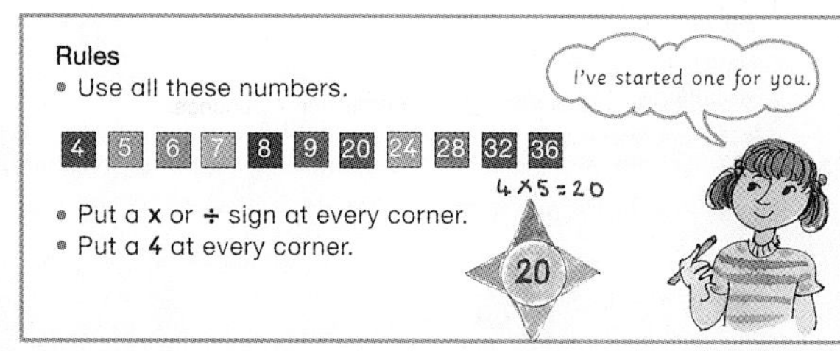

Rules
• Use all these numbers.
4 5 6 7 8 9 20 24 28 32 36
• Put a x or ÷ sign at every corner.
• Put a 4 at every corner.
I've started one for you.
4x5=20
20

2 Copy the arrow diagram and draw the missing arrows.

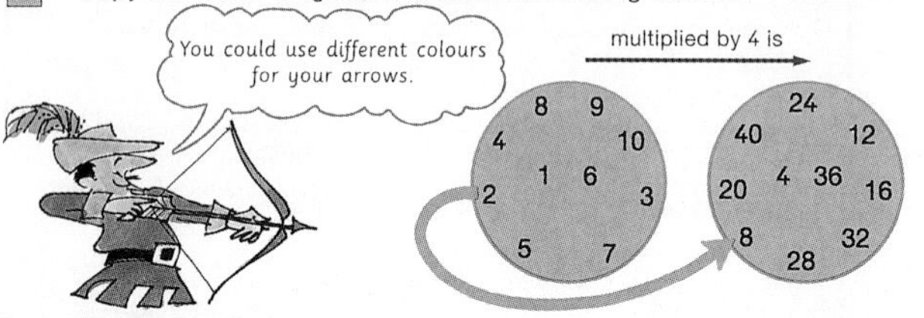

You could use different colours for your arrows.
multiplied by 4 is

CHALLENGE
This machine only outputs numbers larger than 40 written on blue cards.
Draw pairs of input and output cards.
x4

Garden centre

Decide the best way to find the answers to these.
Write down anything that helps.

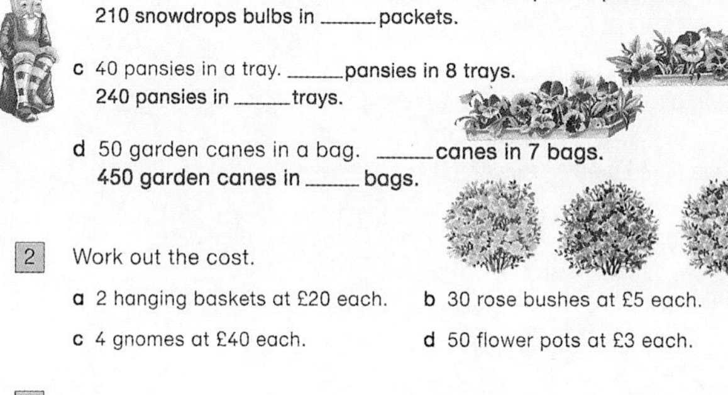

1 Copy and complete the purple sentences.
a 20 daffodils in a bunch. ______ daffodils in 4 bunches.
140 daffodils make ______ bunches.
b 30 snowdrop bulbs in a packet. ______ snowdrops in 6 packets.
210 snowdrops bulbs in ______ packets.
c 40 pansies in a tray. ______ pansies in 8 trays.
240 pansies in ______ trays.
d 50 garden canes in a bag. ______ canes in 7 bags.
450 garden canes in ______ bags.

2 Work out the cost.

a 2 hanging baskets at £20 each. b 30 rose bushes at £5 each.

c 4 gnomes at £40 each. d 50 flower pots at £3 each.

3 Work out how much the garden centre will charge if someone buys all the items in 2.

CHALLENGE
Doug's mum wants to spend £90 on hanging baskets and roses.
Find different ways for her to spend her money.

BOOK 3b PAGE 81

1

4 x 5 = 20	4 x 8 = 32
5 x 4 = 20	8 x 4 = 32
20 ÷ 4 = 5	32 ÷ 4 = 8
20 ÷ 5 = 4	32 ÷ 8 = 4
4 x 6 = 24	4 x 9 = 36
6 x 4 = 24	9 x 4 = 36
24 ÷ 4 = 6	36 ÷ 4 = 9
24 ÷ 6 = 4	36 ÷ 9 = 4
4 x 7 = 28	
7 x 4 = 28	
28 ÷ 4 = 7	
28 ÷ 7 = 4	

Challenge

Open: different ways of combining baskets at £20 each and rose bushes at £5 each to total £90.

For example:
£20 x 3 = £60 and £5 x 6 = £30 making £90 altogether.
(1/3 a,b)

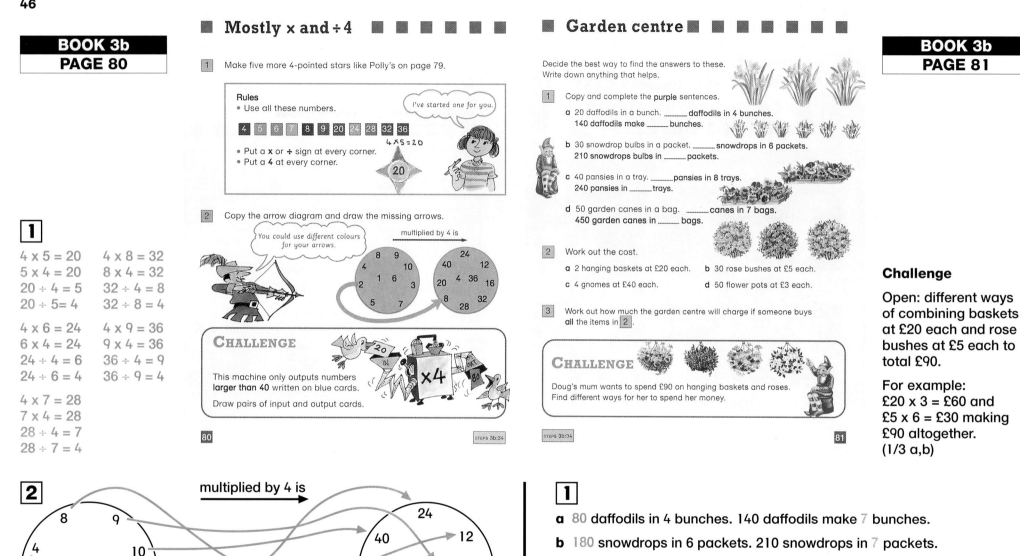

2

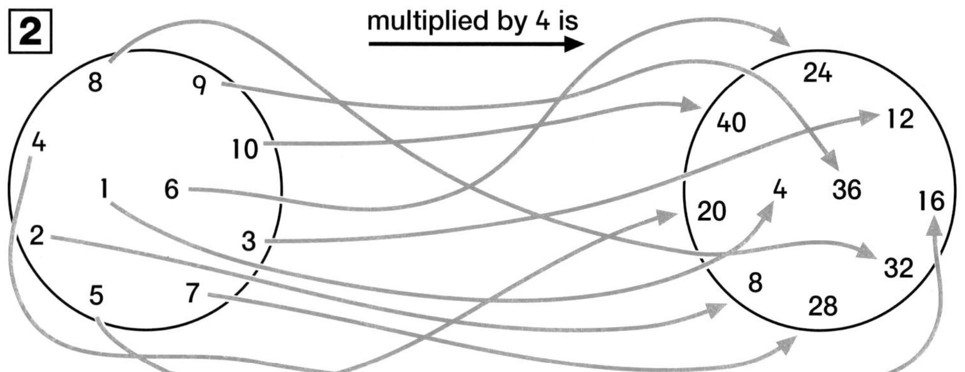

Challenge 11, 44; 12, 48; 13, 52; 14, 56; 15, 60; . . . etc. (1/3 a,b)

1

a 80 daffodils in 4 bunches. 140 daffodils make 7 bunches.

b 180 snowdrops in 6 packets. 210 snowdrops in 7 packets.

c 320 pansies in 8 trays. 240 pansies in 6 trays.

d 350 canes in 7 bags. 450 garden canes in 9 bags.

2

a £40 **b** £150

c £160 **d** £150

3

£500

BOOK 3b
PAGE 82

BOOK 3b
PAGE 83

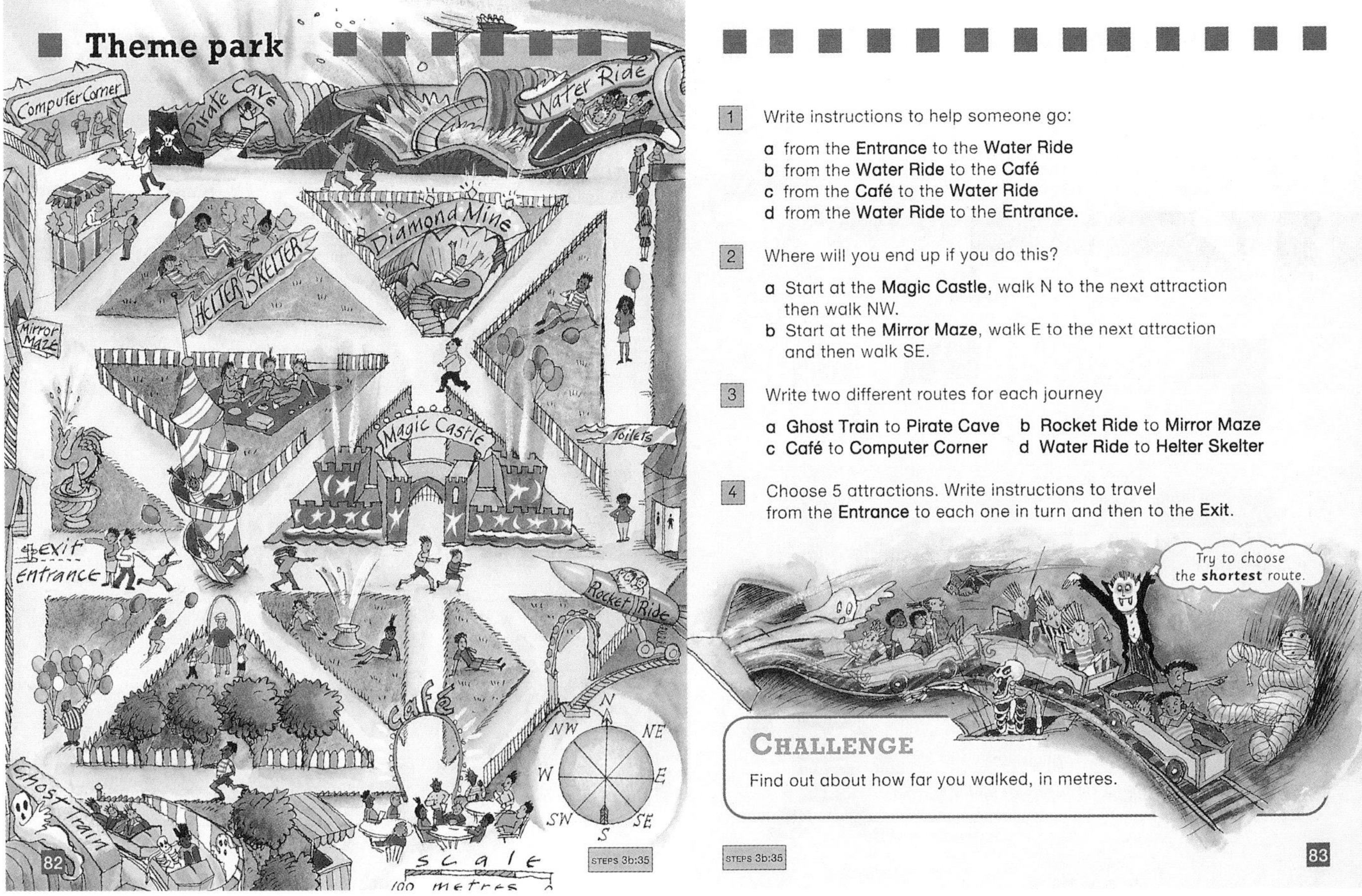

Theme park

1. Write instructions to help someone go:
   - a from the **Entrance** to the **Water Ride**
   - b from the **Water Ride** to the **Café**
   - c from the **Café** to the **Water Ride**
   - d from the **Water Ride** to the **Entrance.**
2. Where will you end up if you do this?
   - a Start at the **Magic Castle**, walk N to the next attraction then walk NW.
   - b Start at the **Mirror Maze**, walk E to the next attraction and then walk SE.
3. Write two different routes for each journey
   - a **Ghost Train** to **Pirate Cave**
   - b **Rocket Ride** to **Mirror Maze**
   - c **Café** to **Computer Corner**
   - d **Water Ride** to **Helter Skelter**
4. Choose 5 attractions. Write instructions to travel from the **Entrance** to each one in turn and then to the **Exit.**

CHALLENGE

Find out about how far you walked, in metres.

1

a East to the Helter Skelter, then North-East to the Water Ride.

b South-West to the Magic Castle, then South to the Café.

c North to the Magic Castle, then North-East to the Water Ride.

d South-West as far as the Helter Skelter, then West to the Entrance.

2

a Pirate Cave **b** Toilets

3

Open: writing two different routes for each of these journeys:

a Ghost Train to Pirate Cave

b Rocket Ride to Mirror Maze

c Café to Computer Corner

d Water Ride to Helter Skelter.

4

Open: instructions for reaching five different attractions from the Entrance and returning to the Exit.

Challenge

Estimating how far walked by using the scale at the bottom right-hand corner of the map. (1/3 a,b,c)

BOOK 3b
PAGE 84

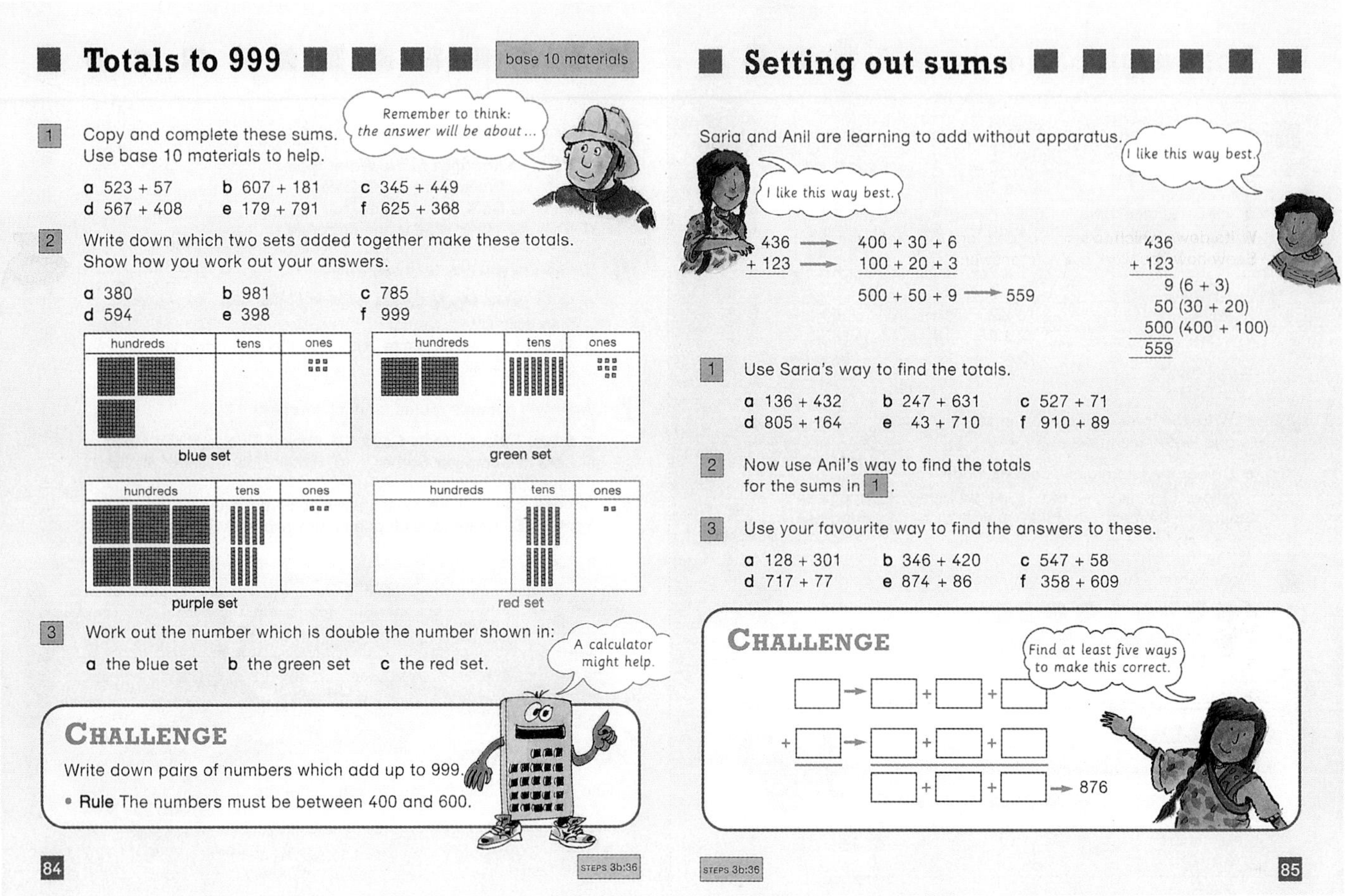

Totals to 999

base 10 materials

Remember to think: *the answer will be about ...*

1 Copy and complete these sums. Use base 10 materials to help.

a 523 + 57 b 607 + 181 c 345 + 449
d 567 + 408 e 179 + 791 f 625 + 368

2 Write down which two sets added together make these totals. Show how you work out your answers.

a 380 b 981 c 785
d 594 e 398 f 999

hundreds	tens	ones

blue set

hundreds	tens	ones

green set

hundreds	tens	ones

purple set

hundreds	tens	ones

red set

3 Work out the number which is double the number shown in:

a the blue set b the green set c the red set.

A calculator might help.

CHALLENGE

Write down pairs of numbers which add up to 999.

- **Rule** The numbers must be between 400 and 600.

84 STEPS 3b:36

BOOK 3b
PAGE 85

Setting out sums

Saria and Anil are learning to add without apparatus.

I like this way best.

436 → 400 + 30 + 6
+ 123 → 100 + 20 + 3
500 + 50 + 9 → 559

I like this way best.

436
+ 123
9 (6 + 3)
50 (30 + 20)
500 (400 + 100)
559

1 Use Saria's way to find the totals.

a 136 + 432 b 247 + 631 c 527 + 71
d 805 + 164 e 43 + 710 f 910 + 89

2 Now use Anil's way to find the totals for the sums in 1.

3 Use your favourite way to find the answers to these.

a 128 + 301 b 346 + 420 c 547 + 58
d 717 + 77 e 874 + 86 f 358 + 609

CHALLENGE

Find at least five ways to make this correct.

□ → □ + □ + □
+ □ → □ + □ + □
□ + □ + □ → 876

STEPS 3b:36 85

1

a 580 b 788 c 794
d 975 e 970 f 993

3

a 612 b 576 c 184

2

a green + red b green + purple
c purple + red d blue + green
e blue + red f blue + purple

Challenge

Find pairs of numbers between 400 and 600 which add up to 999.

For example:
451 + 548 = 999.
(1/3 b)

1

a 136 → 100 + 30 + 6
+ 432 → 400 + 30 + 2
500 + 60 + 8 → 568

b 878 c 598 d 969
e 753 f 999

3

a 429 b 766 c 605
d 794 e 960 f 967

2

a 136
+ 432
8 (2+6)
60 (30+30)
500 (100+400)
568

b 878 c 598
d 969 e 753
f 999

Challenge

Find at least five ways, using method in question 1, to make a total of 876. (1/3 b)

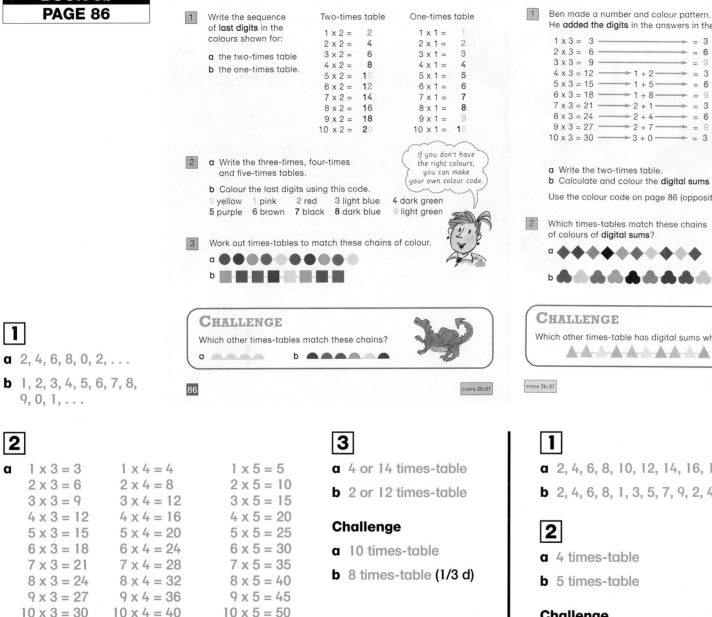

BOOK 3b
PAGE 86

Last-digit patterns

1 Write the sequence of **last digits** in the colours shown for:

a the two-times table
b the one-times table.

Two-times table		One-times table	
1 x 2 =	2	1 x 1 =	1
2 x 2 =	4	2 x 1 =	2
3 x 2 =	6	3 x 1 =	3
4 x 2 =	8	4 x 1 =	4
5 x 2 =	10	5 x 1 =	5
6 x 2 =	12	6 x 1 =	6
7 x 2 =	14	7 x 1 =	7
8 x 2 =	16	8 x 1 =	8
9 x 2 =	18	9 x 1 =	9
10 x 2 =	20	10 x 1 =	10

2 a Write the three-times, four-times and five-times tables.

b Colour the last digits using this code.
0 yellow 1 pink 2 red 3 light blue 4 dark green
5 purple 6 brown 7 black 8 dark blue 9 light green

If you don't have the right colours, you can make your own colour code.

3 Work out times-tables to match these chains of colour.

CHALLENGE
Which other times-tables match these chains?

STEPS 3b:37

BOOK 3b
PAGE 87

Digital sums

1 Ben made a number and colour pattern.
He **added the digits** in the answers in the three-times table.

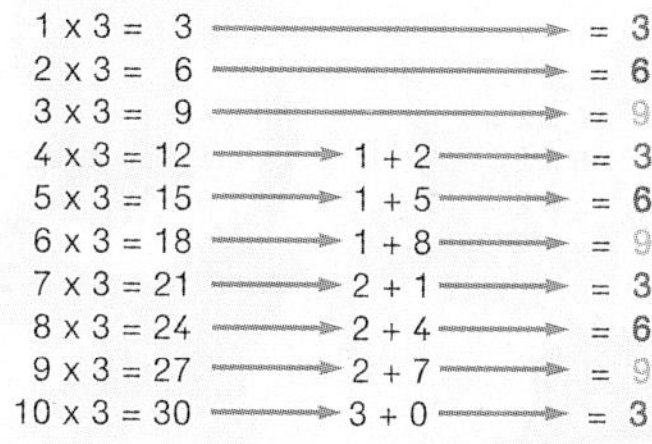

1 x 3 = 3		= 3
2 x 3 = 6		= 6
3 x 3 = 9		= 9
4 x 3 = 12	1 + 2	= 3
5 x 3 = 15	1 + 5	= 6
6 x 3 = 18	1 + 8	= 9
7 x 3 = 21	2 + 1	= 3
8 x 3 = 24	2 + 4	= 6
9 x 3 = 27	2 + 7	= 9
10 x 3 = 30	3 + 0	= 3

Adding the digits in a number is called 'finding the **digital sum**'.

a Write the two-times table.
b Calculate and colour the **digital sums** as Ben did.

Use the colour code on page 86 (opposite).

2 Which times-tables match these chains of colours of **digital sums**?

CHALLENGE
Which other times-table has digital sums which match this chain?

STEPS 3b:37

1

a 2, 4, 6, 8, 0, 2, . . .

b 1, 2, 3, 4, 5, 6, 7, 8, 9, 0, 1, . . .

2

a

1 x 3 = 3	1 x 4 = 4	1 x 5 = 5
2 x 3 = 6	2 x 4 = 8	2 x 5 = 10
3 x 3 = 9	3 x 4 = 12	3 x 5 = 15
4 x 3 = 12	4 x 4 = 16	4 x 5 = 20
5 x 3 = 15	5 x 4 = 20	5 x 5 = 25
6 x 3 = 18	6 x 4 = 24	6 x 5 = 30
7 x 3 = 21	7 x 4 = 28	7 x 5 = 35
8 x 3 = 24	8 x 4 = 32	8 x 5 = 40
9 x 3 = 27	9 x 4 = 36	9 x 5 = 45
10 x 3 = 30	10 x 4 = 40	10 x 5 = 50

b Colour last digits using code.

3

a 4 or 14 times-table

b 2 or 12 times-table

Challenge

a 10 times-table

b 8 times-table **(1/3 d)**

1

a 2, 4, 6, 8, 10, 12, 14, 16, 18, 20, 22, 24, . . .

b 2, 4, 6, 8, 1, 3, 5, 7, 9, 2, 4, 6, . . .

2

a 4 times-table

b 5 times-table

Challenge

6 times-table **(1/3 d)**

BOOK 3b
PAGE 88

BOOK 3b
PAGE 89

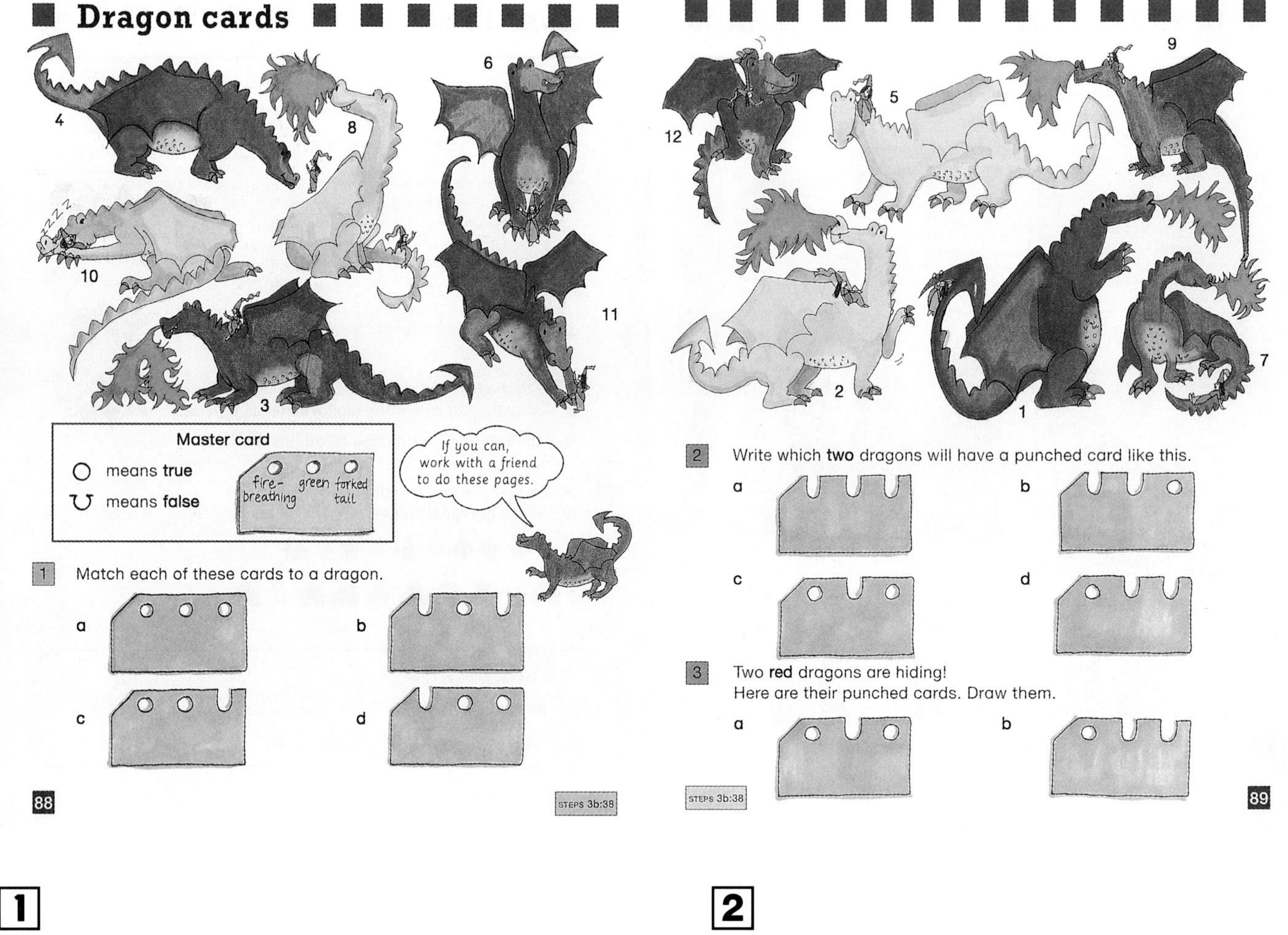

Dragon cards
4
8
6
10
3
11
12
5
9
2
1
7
Master card
○ means true
℧ means false
fire-breathing
green
forked tail
If you can, work with a friend to do these pages.
1 Match each of these cards to a dragon.
a
b
c
d
2 Write which two dragons will have a punched card like this.
a
b
c
d
3 Two red dragons are hiding!
Here are their punched cards. Draw them.
a
b
88
STEPS 3b:38
STEPS 3b:38
89

1

a 3 **b** 12 **c** 9 **d** 6

2

a 10, 11 **b** 4, 5 **c** 1, 2 **d** 7, 8

BOOK 3b
PAGE 90

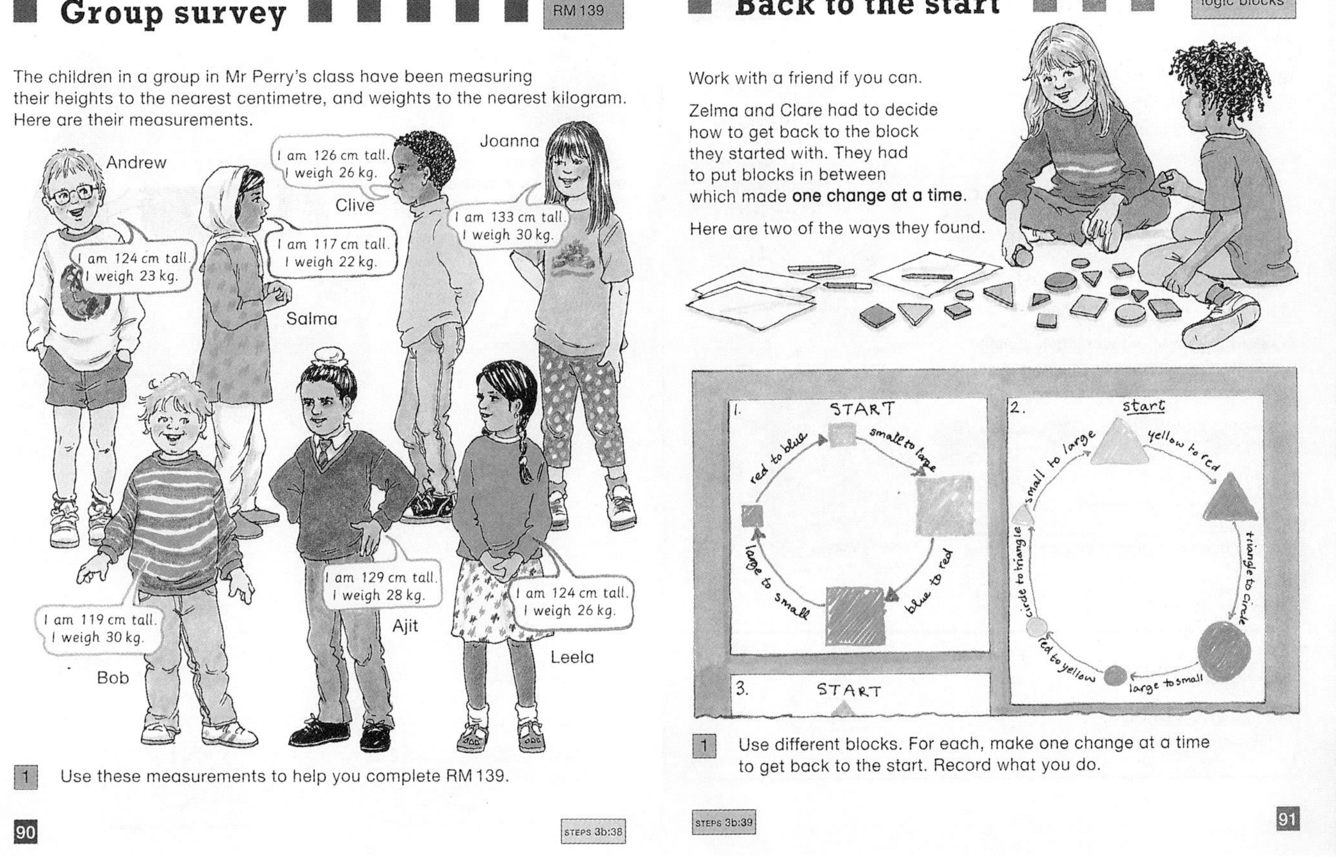

Group survey

RM 139

The children in a group in Mr Perry's class have been measuring their heights to the nearest centimetre, and weights to the nearest kilogram. Here are their measurements.

Andrew
I am 124 cm tall. I weigh 23 kg.
Salma
I am 117 cm tall. I weigh 22 kg.
Clive
I am 126 cm tall. I weigh 26 kg.
Joanna
I am 133 cm tall. I weigh 30 kg.
Bob
I am 119 cm tall. I weigh 30 kg.
Ajit
I am 129 cm tall. I weigh 28 kg.
Leela
I am 124 cm tall. I weigh 26 kg.

1 Use these measurements to help you complete RM 139.

90 STEPS 3b:38

Back to the start

logic blocks

Work with a friend if you can.

Zelma and Clare had to decide how to get back to the block they started with. They had to put blocks in between which made **one change at a time**.

Here are two of the ways they found.

1 Use different blocks. For each, make one change at a time to get back to the start. Record what you do.

STEPS 3b:39 91

BOOK 3b
PAGE 91

1

Complete RM 139 using measurements shown.

1

Open: using different blocks making one change at a time to return to the start and recording the sequence.

BOOK 3b
PAGE 92

One change only

logic blocks

Tim changed a small, blue, thin triangular block into a large, red, thick, circular block.

Then he drew this diagram to show what he did.

Tess did the same but she did it like this!

1. Choose one pair of blocks at a time.
2. In your own way, write down how you change one block into the other.

CHALLENGE

Choose two blocks.
Find and write down different ways of changing one into the other.

92

STEPS 3b:39

1

Open: choosing one pair of blocks.

2

Record how to change from one block to the other making only one change at a time.

Challenge

Open: choosing two blocks and recording different ways of changing from one to the other.
(1/3 a,b,c,d)

RESOURCE MASTERS

RESOURCE MASTER 3

Practical: playing the games.

RESOURCE MASTER 4

Practical: constructing plumb-line.

2

Practical: constructing spirit-level.

RESOURCE MASTER 5

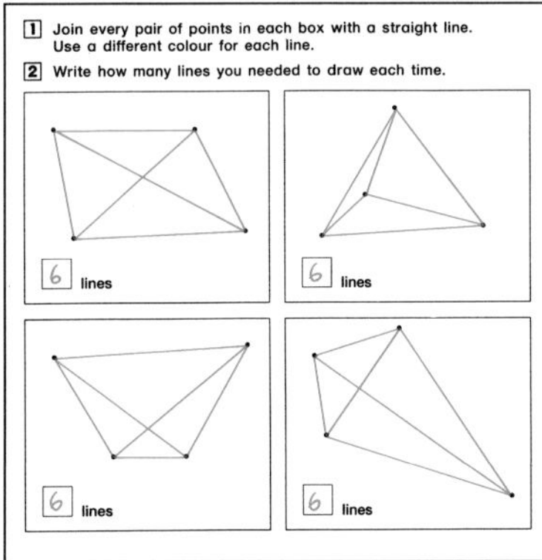

3

Open: children's conclusions after completing questions 1 and 2. (1/3 b)

RESOURCE MASTER 6

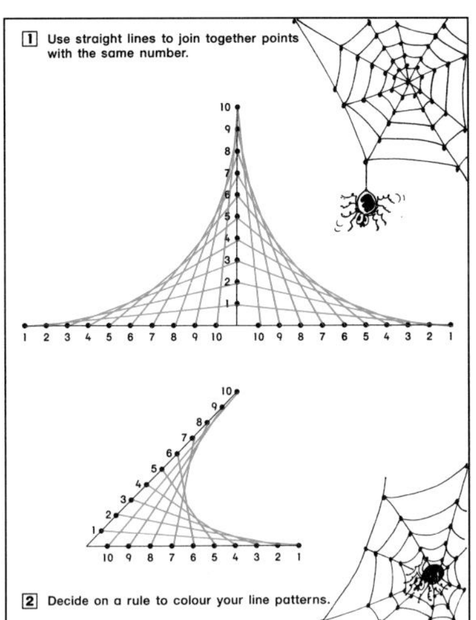

1 Use straight lines to join together points with the same number.
2 Decide on a rule to colour your line patterns.

RESOURCE MASTER 8

Practical: playing the games.

RESOURCE MASTER 10

Practical: playing the games.

RESOURCE MASTER 11

Practical: dice multiplication.

Challenge

Highest product is 40, lowest product is 5.

a 14 x 5 = 70
4 x 5 = 20
10 x 5 = 50

b 22 x 6 = 132
2 x 6 = 12
20 x 6 = 120

c 38 x 4 = 152
8 x 4 = 32
30 x 4 = 120

RESOURCE MASTER 12

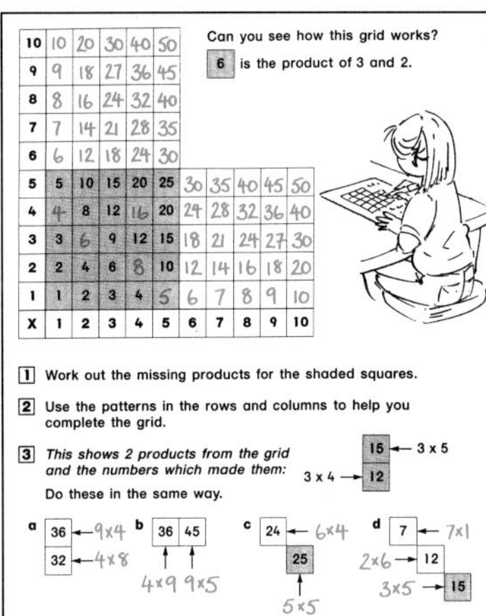

1 Work out the missing products for the shaded squares.

4

Open: more examples like 3 using the grid. (1/3 a,c,d)

RESOURCE MASTER 13

1 x 1 = 1
5 x 2 = 10
0 x 5 = 0
4 x 4 = 16

2 x 1 = 2
5 x 5 = 25
1 x 3 = 3
4 x 2 = 8

5 x 1 = 5
2 x 3 = 6
5 x 3 = 15
2 x 2 = 4

4 x 5 = 20
3 x 4 = 12
3 x 3 = 9
1 x 4 = 4

a 36 **b** 24 **c** 28

4

a 75 **b** 108

RESOURCE MASTER 14

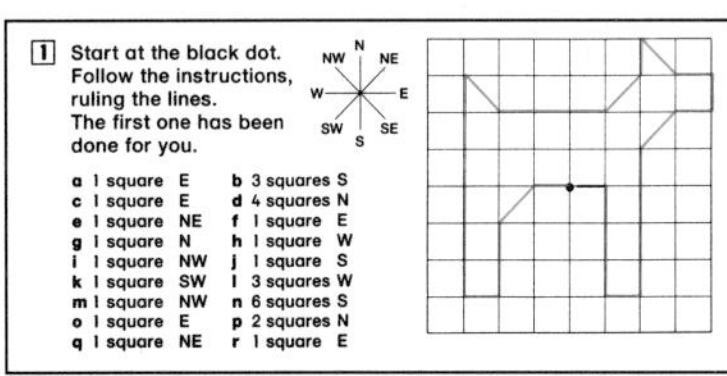

1 Start at the black dot. Follow the instructions, ruling the lines. The first one has been done for you.

2 **3**

Draw picture on grid, write instructions on how to construct the picture.

4

Open: swap instructions from 3 with friend and draw each other's picture. (1/3 a,c,d)

RESOURCE MASTER 17

Open: own additions with numbers up to 999. (1/3 b,c)

RESOURCE MASTER 18

a 335 + 123 = 458
b 253 + 243 = 496
c 172 + 116 = 288
d 300 + 135 = 435
e 100 + 400 = 500
f 444 + 51 = 495

2

a + b = 185
a + c = 227
a + d = 456
b + c = 168
b + d = 397
c + d = 439

RESOURCE MASTER 19

1

a 53 **b** 148
c 132 **d** 141
e 32 **f** 234

3

a 104 + 20 = 124
124 + 20 = 144
144 + 20 = 164
164 + 20 = 184
184 + 20 = 204
204 + 20 = 224
224 + 20 = 244
244 + 20 = 264
264 + 20 = 284
284 + 20 = 304

b 201 + 0 = 201
201 + 10 = 211
201 + 20 = 221
201 + 30 = 231
201 + 40 = 241
201 + 50 = 251
201 + 60 = 261
201 + 70 = 271
201 + 80 = 281
201 + 90 = 301

c Open: own addition patterns up to 999. (1/3 b,c)

RESOURCE MASTER 20

1

a 178 **b** 94
c 311 **d** 496
e 250 **f** 432
g 312

2

rounds off to

36 → 40
57 → 60
29 → 30
302 → 300
163 → 160
195 → 200

will have a total of about

36 + 57 → 40 + 60 → 100
163 + 29 → 160 + 30 → 190
195 + 29 → 200 + 30 → 230
57 + 302 → 60 + 300 → 360
195 + 302 → 200 + 300 → 500
36 + 163 → 40 + 160 → 200
163 + 195 → 160 + 200 → 360

RESOURCE MASTER 21

83
100
324
520
409
117
202
641
971

2

Open: complete the table.

RESOURCE MASTER 22

1

b

IN	OUT
6	11
15	20
10	15

c

IN	OUT
17	15
13	11
20	18

d

IN	OUT
16	26
32	42
105	115

e

IN	OUT
6	12
9	18
5	10

RESOURCE MASTER 23

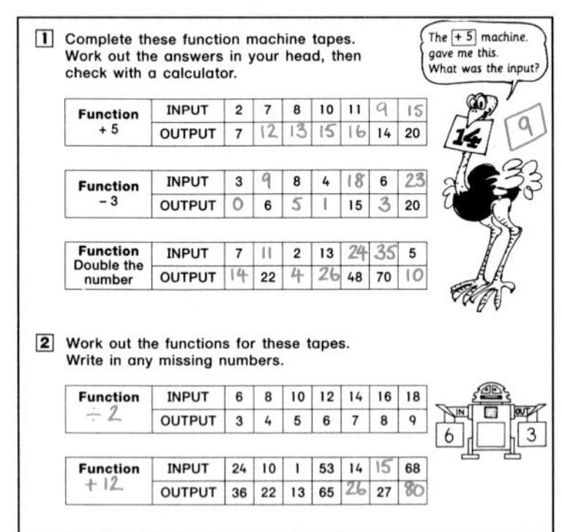

1 Complete these function machine tapes. Work out the answers in your head, then check with a calculator.

Function + 5	INPUT	2	7	8	10	11	9	15
	OUTPUT	7	12	13	15	16	14	20

Function − 3	INPUT	3	9	8	4	18	6	23
	OUTPUT	0	6	5	1	15	3	20

Function Double the number	INPUT	7	11	2	13	24	35	5
	OUTPUT	14	22	4	26	48	70	10

2 Work out the functions for these tapes. Write in any missing numbers.

Function ÷ 2	INPUT	6	8	10	12	14	16	18
	OUTPUT	3	4	5	6	7	8	9

Function + 12	INPUT	24	10	1	53	14	15	68
	OUTPUT	36	22	13	65	26	27	80

RESOURCE MASTER 24

18, 31, 58, 109, 74, 116, 85

2

0, 55, 41, 85, 29, 94, 336, 400

3

10, 70, 20, 35, 65 100, 50, 45

4

1, 4, 6, 14, 12, 20, 22, 7

RESOURCE MASTER 27

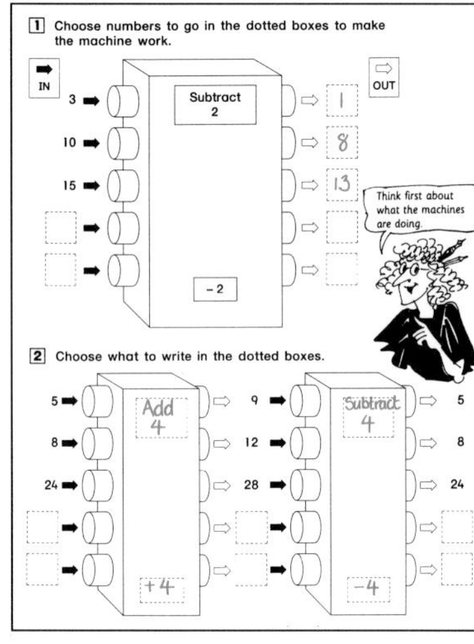

RESOURCE MASTER 28

Practical: playing the game.

RESOURCE MASTER 29

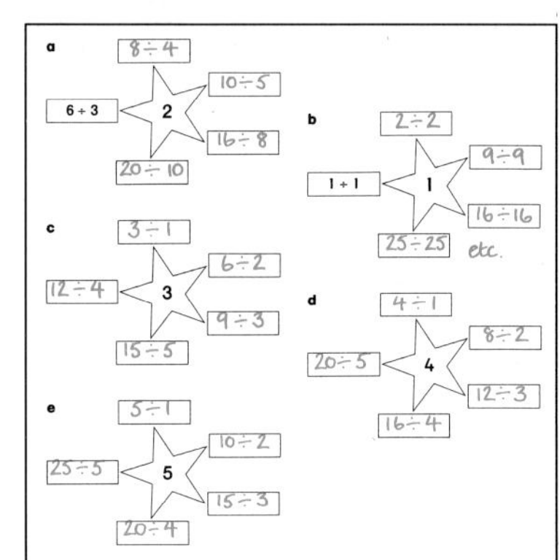

RESOURCE MASTER 30

1 Complete the patterns in the grids below. Choose materials to help you.

2 Stop each pattern when you get an answer of 10.

3 Keep this sheet safe to help you check division facts.

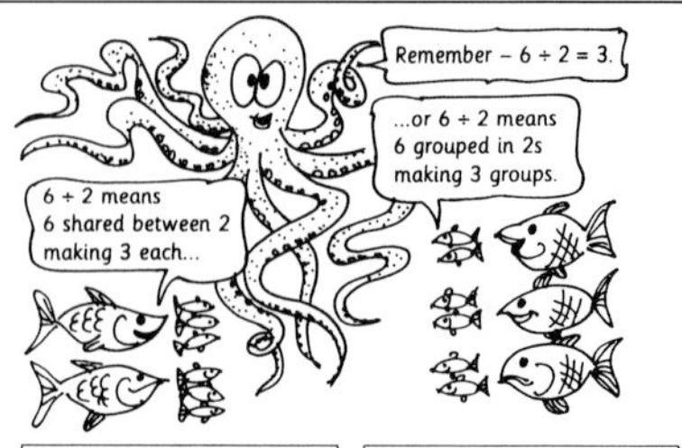

a ÷ 2	**b** ÷ 3	**c** ÷ 4	**d** ÷ 5
2 ÷ 2 = 1	3 ÷ 3 = 1	4 ÷ 4 = 1	5 ÷ 5 = 1
4 ÷ 2 = 2	6 ÷ 3 = 2	8 ÷ 4 = 2	10 ÷ 5 = 2
6 ÷ 2 = 3	9 ÷ 3 = 3	12 ÷ 4 = 3	15 ÷ 5 = 3
8 ÷ 2 = 4	12 ÷ 3 = 4	16 ÷ 4 = 4	20 ÷ 5 = 4
10 ÷ 2 = 5	15 ÷ 3 = 5	20 ÷ 4 = 5	25 ÷ 5 = 5
12 ÷ 2 = 6	18 ÷ 3 = 6	24 ÷ 4 = 6	30 ÷ 5 = 6
14 ÷ 2 = 7	21 ÷ 3 = 7	28 ÷ 4 = 7	35 ÷ 5 = 7
16 ÷ 2 = 8	24 ÷ 3 = 8	32 ÷ 4 = 8	40 ÷ 5 = 8
18 ÷ 2 = 9	27 ÷ 3 = 9	36 ÷ 4 = 9	45 ÷ 5 = 9
20 ÷ 2 = 10	30 ÷ 3 = 10	40 ÷ 4 = 10	50 ÷ 5 = 10

RESOURCE MASTER 31

a 13 ÷ 2 = 6 remainder 1
b 17 ÷ 2 = 8 remainder 1
c 19 ÷ 2 = 9 remainder 1
d 25 ÷ 3 = 8 remainder 1
e 17 ÷ 3 = 5 remainder 2
f 20 ÷ 3 = 6 remainder 2

3

a 17 ÷ 4 = 4 remainder 1
b 26 ÷ 4 = 6 remainder 2
c 31 ÷ 4 = 7 remainder 3
d 27 ÷ 5 = 5 remainder 2
e 31 ÷ 5 = 6 remainder 1
f 39 ÷ 5 = 7 remainder 4

2

Open: check answers by grouping.

Open: write a sharing story about 23 ÷ 4.

5

Open: draw a grouping picture for 28 ÷ 5.

30 ÷ 3 = 10, 30 ÷ 5 = 6,
30 ÷ 6 = 5, 30 ÷ 10 = 3,
30 ÷ 15 = 2, 30 ÷ 30 = 1

RESOURCE MASTER 32

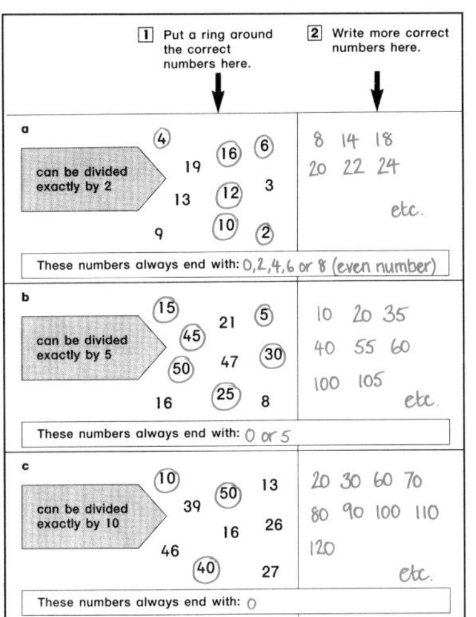

1 Put a ring around the correct numbers here.
2 Write more correct numbers here.
a can be divided exactly by 2

These numbers always end with: 0,2,4,6 or 8 (even number)
b can be divided exactly by 5

These numbers always end with: 0 or 5
c can be divided exactly by 10

These numbers always end with: 0

RESOURCE MASTER 33

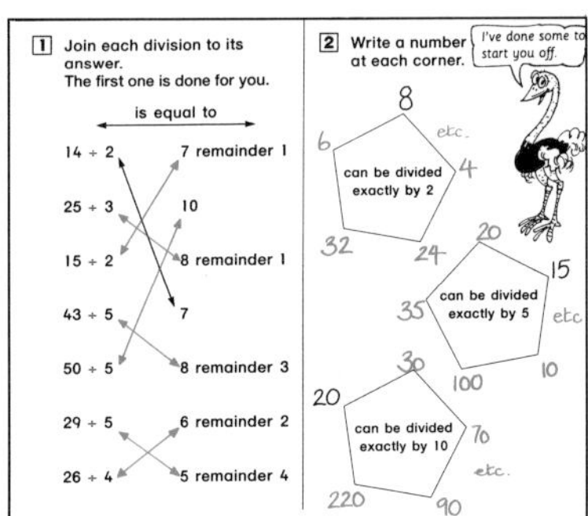

is equal to

2 Write a number at each corner.

can be divided exactly by 2
can be divided exactly by 5
can be divided exactly by 10

3

4 ÷ 2 = 2
6 ÷ 3 = 2
8 ÷ 4 = 2
10 ÷ 5 = 2
12 ÷ 2 = 6
20 ÷ 10 = 2

RESOURCE MASTER 34

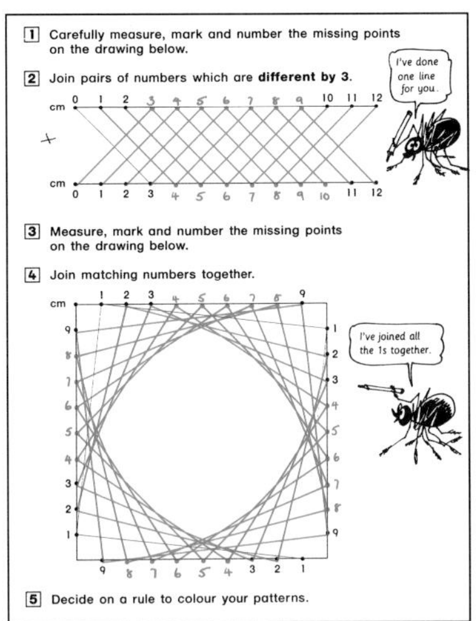

1 Carefully measure, mark and number the missing points on the drawing below.
2 Join pairs of numbers which are different by 3.
I've done one line for you.
3 Measure, mark and number the missing points on the drawing below.
4 Join matching numbers together.
I've joined all the 1s together.
5 Decide on a rule to colour your patterns.

RESOURCE MASTER 35

Open: working in groups, estimating and measuring. (1/4 a)

RESOURCE MASTER 36

Practical: cards should be placed along the length line in the following order:

5 cm, 24 cm, 52 cm, 77 cm, 90 cm, 2 m 0 cm, 2 m 13 cm, 2 m 40 cm, 2 m 50 cm, 2 m 61cm, 2 m 75 cm, 2 m 80 cm, 3 m 0 cm, 3 m 5 cm, 3 m 10 cm, 3 m 40 cm, 3 m 76 cm, 3 m 99 cm, 4 m 0 cm, 4 m cm, 4 m 25 cm, 4 m 35 cm, 4 m 70 cm, 5 m 0 cm.

RESOURCE MASTER 37

1 Complete this table.

Length in centimetres (cm)	Length in decimetres (dm)	Length in metres (m)
20 cm	2 dm	0·2 m
90 cm	9dm	0·9m
30 cm	3dm	0·3m
60cm	6 dm	0·6m
100 cm	10 dm	1·0 m
40cm	4 dm	0·4m
70 cm	7dm	0·7m
10 cm	1dm	0·1 m
80 cm	8 dm	0·8m
50 cm	5dm	0·5 m

2

a 0.8m
b 0.5 m
c 0.6 m
d 0.1 m
e 0.3 m
f 0.9 m

RESOURCE MASTER 38

Practical: measuring and estimating.

RESOURCE MASTER 39

1

b 2m 36 cm
c 290 cm
d Several possibilities
e Several possibilities

2

b 1.3 m
c Several possibilities
d 320 cm
e Several possibilities

3

b 120 cm
c Between 226 and 234
d Several possibilities

4

Open: measuring and estimating the length of objects.

RESOURCE MASTER 40

Open: rearranging cards to show the same figures.

RESOURCE MASTER 41

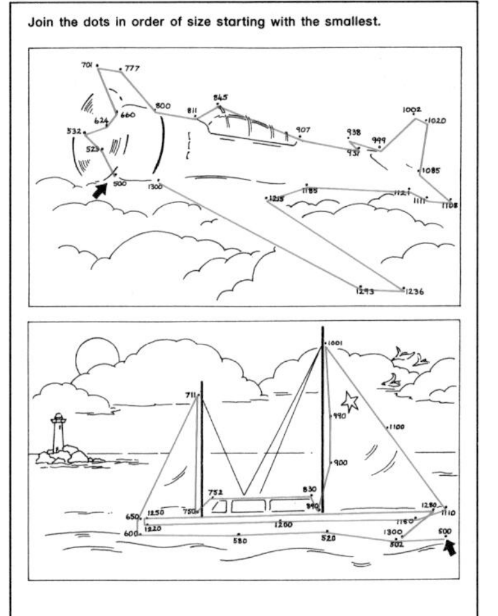

Join the dots in order of size starting with the smallest.

RESOURCE MASTER 42

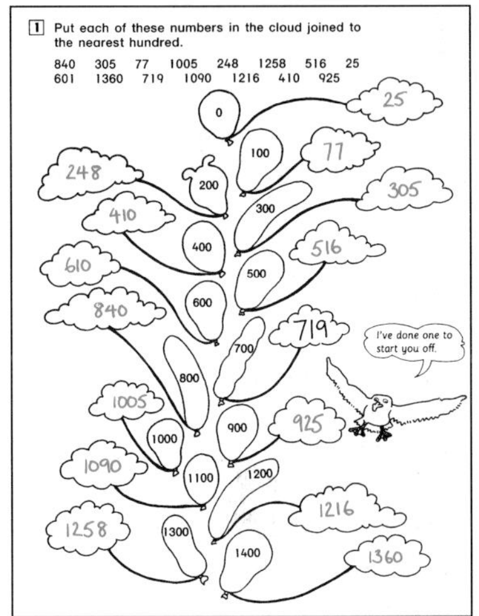

1 Put each of these numbers in the cloud joined to the nearest hundred.
840 305 77 1005 248 1258 516 25
601 1360 719 1090 1216 410 925

RESOURCE MASTER 43

1

a 15 – 4 = 11
25 – 4 = 21
35 – 4 = 31
45 – 4 = 41
55 – 4 = 51
65 – 4 = 61
75 – 4 = 71
85 – 4 = 81
95 – 4 = 91

b 20 – 17 = 3
30 – 27 = 3
40 – 37 = 3
50 – 47 = 3
60 – 57 = 3
70 – 67 = 3
80 – 77 = 3
90 – 87 = 3

c 99 – 5 = 94
99 – 15 = 84
99 – 25 = 74
99 – 35 = 64
99 – 45 = 54
99 – 55 = 44
99 – 65 = 34
99 – 75 = 24
99 – 85 = 14
99 – 95 = 4

2

Open: own subtraction patterns with numbers upto 100. (1/3 b,c)

RESOURCE MASTER 44

Open: own 'take-away' problems up to 999. (1/3 b,c)

RESOURCE MASTER 45

Open: systematic subtraction using flow diagram.

RESOURCE MASTER 46

1

a 158 **b** 77
c 157 **d** 289
e 154 **f** 163

Many possibilities

RESOURCE MASTER 47

1

Many possibilities

2

a 31

b 20

c 110

d 53

e 100

f 244

g Many possibilities

h Many possibilities

RESOURCE MASTER 48

1

68 cm shorter

2

191 children

3

92 different

4

175 g

Challenge

24 marbles

RESOURCE MASTER 49

1

b 342 – 117 = 225

$$\begin{array}{r} 225 \\ +\ 117 \\ \hline 342 \end{array}$$

c 209 – 132 = 77

$$\begin{array}{r} 77 \\ +\ 132 \\ \hline 209 \end{array}$$

d 422 – 257 = 165

$$\begin{array}{r} 165 \\ +\ 257 \\ \hline 422 \end{array}$$

2

a 92 – 71 = 21

$$\begin{array}{r} 21 \\ +\ 71 \\ \hline 92 \end{array}$$

b 345 – 229 = 16

$$\begin{array}{r} 16 \\ +\ 229 \\ \hline 245 \end{array}$$

c 214 – 68 = 156

$$\begin{array}{r} 156 \\ +\ 68 \\ \hline 224 \end{array}$$

d 454 – 327 = 127

$$\begin{array}{r} 127 \\ +\ 327 \\ \hline 454 \end{array}$$

3

Open: write a story.

RESOURCE MASTER 50

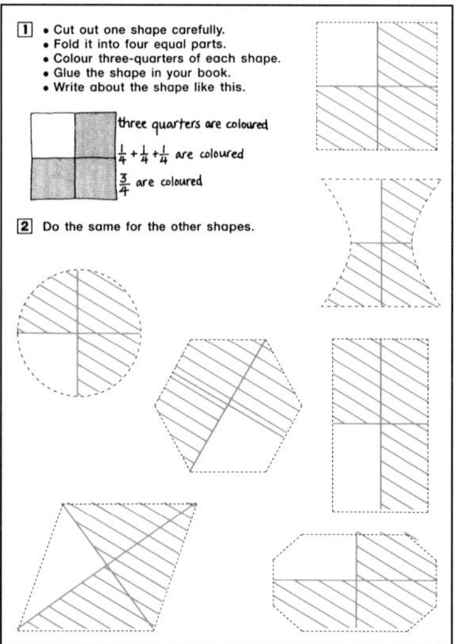
1 • Cut out one shape carefully.
• Fold it into four equal parts.
• Colour three-quarters of each shape.
• Glue the shape in your book.
• Write about the shape like this.

three quarters are coloured
$\frac{1}{4}+\frac{1}{4}+\frac{1}{4}$ are coloured
$\frac{3}{4}$ are coloured

2 Do the same for the other shapes.

RESOURCE MASTER 51

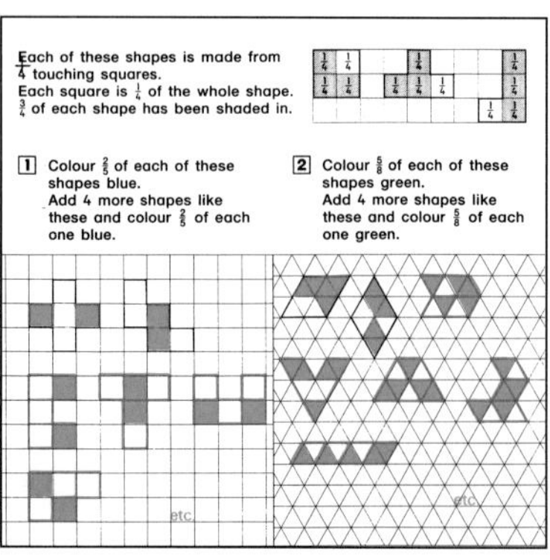
Each of these shapes is made from 4 touching squares.
Each square is $\frac{1}{4}$ of the whole shape.
$\frac{3}{4}$ of each shape has been shaded in.

1 Colour $\frac{3}{4}$ of each of these shapes blue. Add 4 more shapes like these and colour $\frac{3}{4}$ of each one blue.

2 Colour $\frac{3}{4}$ of each of these shapes green. Add 4 more shapes like these and colour $\frac{3}{4}$ of each one green.

RESOURCE MASTER 52

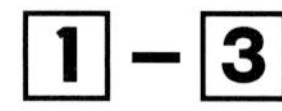

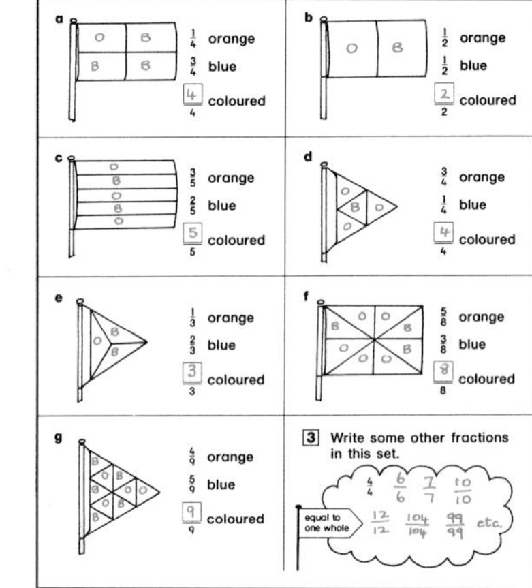
a $\frac{1}{4}$ orange $\frac{3}{4}$ blue $\frac{4}{4}$ coloured
b $\frac{1}{2}$ orange $\frac{1}{2}$ blue $\frac{2}{2}$ coloured
c $\frac{3}{5}$ orange $\frac{2}{5}$ blue $\frac{5}{5}$ coloured
d $\frac{3}{4}$ orange $\frac{1}{4}$ blue $\frac{4}{4}$ coloured
e $\frac{1}{3}$ orange $\frac{2}{3}$ blue $\frac{3}{3}$ coloured
f $\frac{5}{8}$ orange $\frac{3}{8}$ blue $\frac{8}{8}$ coloured
g $\frac{4}{9}$ orange $\frac{5}{9}$ blue $\frac{9}{9}$ coloured

3 Write some other fractions in this set.
equal to one whole
etc.

RESOURCE MASTER 53

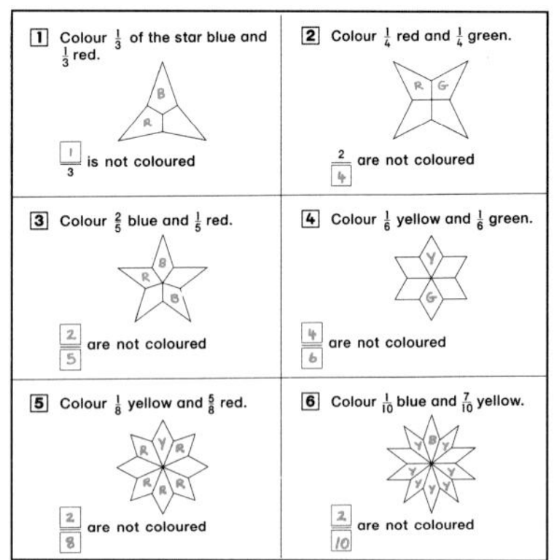
1 Colour $\frac{1}{3}$ of the star blue and $\frac{1}{3}$ red.
$\frac{1}{3}$ is not coloured
2 Colour $\frac{1}{4}$ red and $\frac{1}{4}$ green.
$\frac{2}{4}$ are not coloured
3 Colour $\frac{2}{5}$ blue and $\frac{1}{5}$ red.
$\frac{2}{5}$ are not coloured
4 Colour $\frac{1}{6}$ yellow and $\frac{1}{6}$ green.
$\frac{4}{6}$ are not coloured
5 Colour $\frac{1}{8}$ yellow and $\frac{5}{8}$ red.
$\frac{2}{8}$ are not coloured
6 Colour $\frac{1}{10}$ blue and $\frac{7}{10}$ yellow.
$\frac{2}{10}$ are not coloured

7

a $\frac{2}{3}$

b $\frac{5}{8}$

c $\frac{4}{5}$

d $\frac{9}{10}$

e $\frac{3}{4}$

f $\frac{9}{10}$

8

a $\frac{2}{5}$

b $\frac{3}{4}$

c $\frac{3}{10}$

d $\frac{4}{8}$

e $\frac{3}{5}$

f $\frac{4}{6}$

RESOURCE MASTER 54

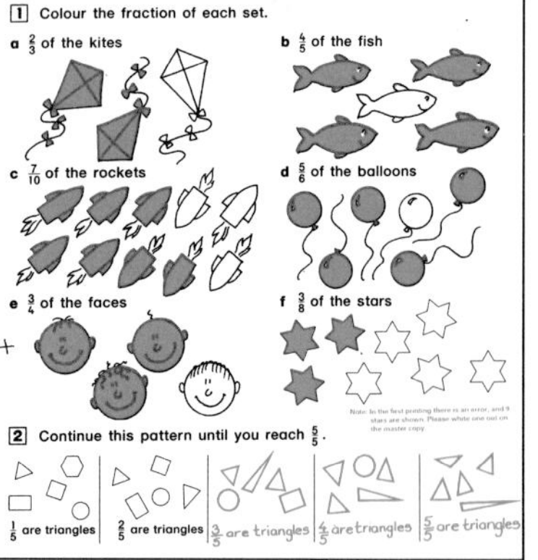
1 Colour the fraction of each set.
a $\frac{2}{3}$ of the kites
b $\frac{4}{5}$ of the fish
c $\frac{7}{10}$ of the rockets
d $\frac{5}{6}$ of the balloons
e $\frac{3}{4}$ of the faces
f $\frac{3}{8}$ of the stars

2 Continue this pattern until you reach $\frac{5}{5}$.
$\frac{1}{5}$ are triangles
$\frac{2}{5}$ are triangles
$\frac{3}{5}$ are triangles
$\frac{4}{5}$ are triangles
$\frac{5}{5}$ are triangles

3

Open: recognising fractions of a set. (1/3 b,c)

RESOURCE MASTER 55

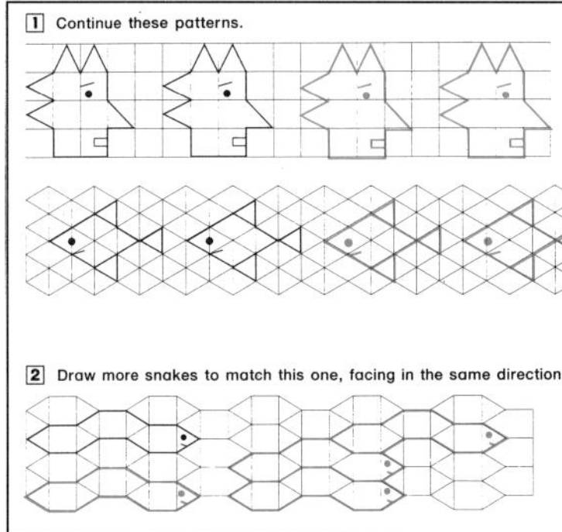

3

Open: make up own patterns. (1/3 b)

RESOURCE MASTER 56

Practical: play the game.

RESOURCE MASTER 58

Open: finding co-ordinates (1/3 b)

RESOURCE MASTER 59

Maths is great.

2

Where do bees go for transport? The buzz stop.

3

C2 C5 A6 E3 E1 D6 E4 E1 C6 A6 E3 D3 E1 E6 A6 E3 E1 A5 E4 C3 E1 B5 C3 E6 A6 A4 A5 A6 D3 E3 D1 C4 D5 C6 E6 E1 C6 C3 D5 D3 A3 E6 D3 B1

4

Open: write a joke in code.

RESOURCE MASTER 60

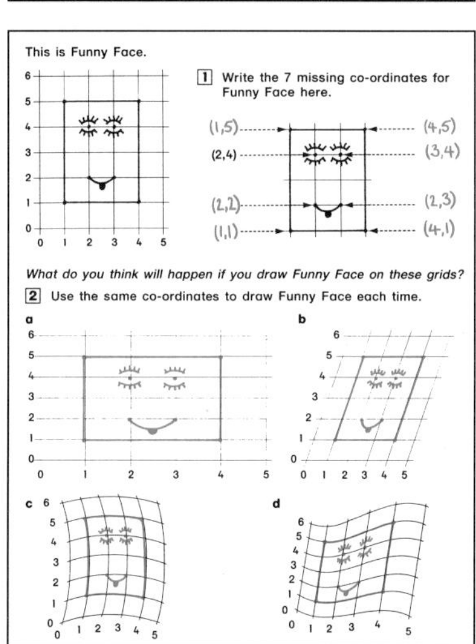

RESOURCE MASTER 63

a 5 x 5 x 4
Perimeter = 14 cm

b 4 x 6 x 5
Perimeter = 15 cm

c 2 x 7 x 2 x 7
Perimeter = 18 cm

d 3 x 3 x 4 x 6
Perimeter = 16 cm

e 1 x 4 x 2 x 6
Perimeter = 13 cm

f 2 x 6 x 2 x 2 x 1 x 5
Perimeter = 18 cm

RESOURCE MASTER 64

Open: estimates will vary.

2

a 9 **b** 7 **c** 21 **d** 8 **e** 10

3

c, e, a, d, b

RESOURCE MASTER 65

Open: balancing multiples of 10 grams. (1/3 a,b)

RESOURCE MASTER 66

1 How many different ways can you make 100 grams? Complete the chart with your ideas.

50 g	20 g	10 g	5 g	1 g
2	0	0	0	0
1	2	1	0	0
1	2	0	2	0
1	2	0	0	10
1	2	0	1	5
1	1	3	0	0
1	1	1	2	0
1	1	1	2	10
1	1	1	1	15
0	5	0	0	0
0	4	2	0	0
0	4	1	2	0
1	0	5	0	0
0	3	3	2	0
1	0	0	10	0
0	2	5	1	5

We've done the first one for you!

100g balances

Some possible examples

etc.

RESOURCE MASTER 67

Practical: play the game.

RESOURCE MASTER 68

a 65p → £0.65

b 103p → £1.03

c 1050p → £10.50

2

a 20p **b** 20p

c £1 **d** 60p

e £1.40 **f** £10.10

3

a £2 **b** £7

c £11 **d** £23

4

a 7p **b** 70p

c £7 **d** 7p

4

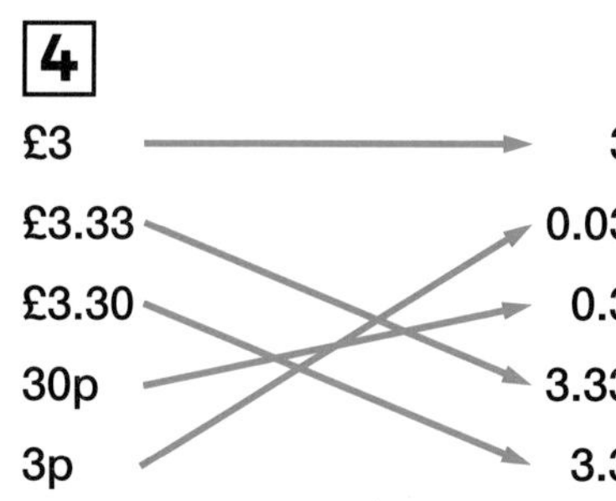

RESOURCE MASTER 70

b

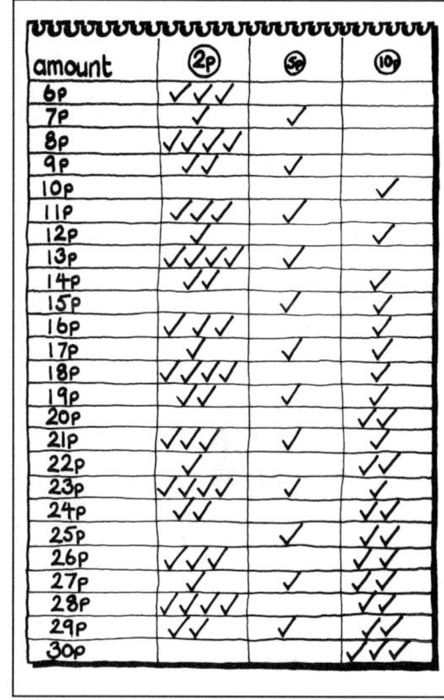

amount	2p	5p	10p
6p	✓✓✓		
7p	✓	✓	
8p	✓✓✓✓		
9p	✓✓	✓	
10p			✓
11p	✓✓✓	✓	
12p	✓		✓
13p	✓✓✓✓	✓	
14p	✓✓		✓
15p		✓	✓
16p	✓✓✓		✓
17p	✓	✓	✓
18p	✓✓✓✓		✓
19p	✓✓	✓	✓
20p			✓✓
21p	✓✓✓	✓	✓
22p	✓		✓✓
23p	✓✓✓✓	✓	✓
24p	✓✓		✓✓
25p		✓	✓✓
26p	✓✓✓		✓✓
27p	✓	✓	✓✓
28p	✓✓✓✓		✓✓
29p	✓✓	✓	✓✓
30p			✓✓✓

c 10p, 12p, 14p, 15p, 16p, 17p, 18p, 20p, 21p, 22p, 23p, 24p, 25p, 26p, 27p, 28p, 29p, 30p

d 1p, 3p

2

£6.50, £6.20, £5.70, £1.70

3

£15.50	£10, £5, 50p
£21.20	impossible
£5.40	£5, 20p, 20p
£0.65	impossible

RESOURCE MASTER 71

Practical: play the game.

RESOURCE MASTER 72

Open: estimating and finding volumes by counting cubes. (1/3 a,c)

RESOURCE MASTER 73

Practical: creating a spiral from a circle.

RESOURCE MASTER 74

Practical: learning about radius and diameter by construction.

RESOURCE MASTER 75

Open: using and interpreting language associated with a circle (radius, diameter).

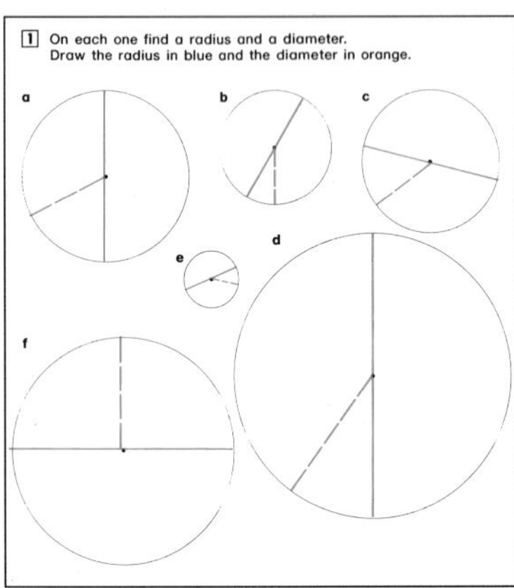

2

Yes. (1/3 b,d)

RESOURCE MASTER 76

Practical: creating circle patterns.

RESOURCE MASTER 77

Practical: interpreting instructions to make a cone.

RESOURCE MASTER 78

Open: making symmetrical halves whole.

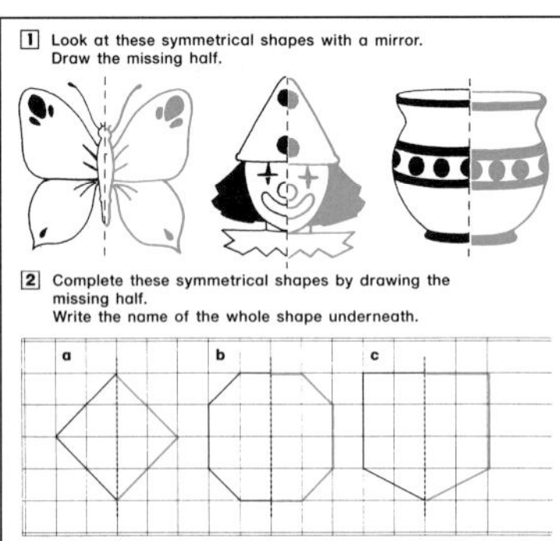

Open: own symetrical shapes.
(1/3 a,b)

RESOURCE MASTER 80

Open: cards could be in this order:

Next birthday I will be a year younger.

I will see a tiger in my garden tonight.

My friends will laugh at my next joke.

I will go swimming next week.

I will need larger shoes next year.

April will be the fourth month next year.

Open: order and write own statements.

RESOURCE MASTER 81

Open: making predictions based on experience and testing them. (1/3 b,d)

RESOURCE MASTER 82

Open: testing and making predictions where two outcomes are equally likely. (1/3 b,c,d)

RESOURCE MASTER 83

Open: identifying and checking who is likely to win a game and why. (1/3 d)

RESOURCE MASTER 84

Open: estimating likelihood: colouring hexagon segments. (1/3 a,b,d)

a ... you have a **very good chance** of spinning blue.	b ... it is **impossible** to spin red.	c ... you are **just as likely** to spin red or yellow.
d ... you are **very unlikely** to spin blue.	e ... you are **certain** to spin yellow every time.	f ... you have an **even chance** of getting blue or red.

RESOURCE MASTER 85

Open: play the game.

Is the game fair or unfair?
Fair.

Why?
Both paths have the same number of spaces, and both also have one unsafe and one safe space.

RESOURCE MASTER 86

Table of 2s	x2 table
2 x 1 = 2	1 x 2 = 2
2 x 2 = 4	2 x 2 = 4
2 x 3 = 6	3 x 2 = 6
2 x 4 = 8	4 x 2 = 8
2 x 5 = 10	5 x 2 = 10
2 x 6 = 12	6 x 2 = 12
2 x 7 = 14	7 x 2 = 14
2 x 8 = 16	8 x 2 = 16
2 x 9 = 18	9 x 2 = 18
2 x 10 = 20	10 x 2 = 20

Table of 5s	x5 table
5 x 1 = 5	1 x 5 = 5
5 x 2 = 10	2 x 5 = 10
5 x 3 = 15	3 x 5 = 15
5 x 4 = 20	4 x 5 = 20
5 x 5 = 25	5 x 5 = 25
5 x 6 = 30	6 x 5 = 30
5 x 7 = 35	7 x 5 = 35
5 x 8 = 40	8 x 5 = 40
5 x 9 = 45	9 x 5 = 45
5 x 10 = 50	10 x 5 = 50

Table of 10s	x10 table
10 x 1 = 10	1 x 10 = 10
10 x 2 = 20	2 x 10 = 20
10 x 3 = 30	3 x 10 = 30
10 x 4 = 40	4 x 10 = 40
10 x 5 = 50	5 x 10 = 50
10 x 6 = 60	6 x 10 = 60
10 x 7 = 70	7 x 10 = 70
10 x 8 = 80	8 x 10 = 80
10 x 9 = 90	9 x 10 = 90
10 x 10 = 100	10 x 10 = 100

RESOURCE MASTER 87

Open: play the game.

RESOURCE MASTER 88

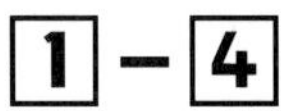

Open: making and sorting cards from 1 to 100.

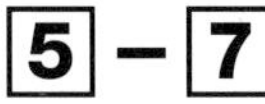

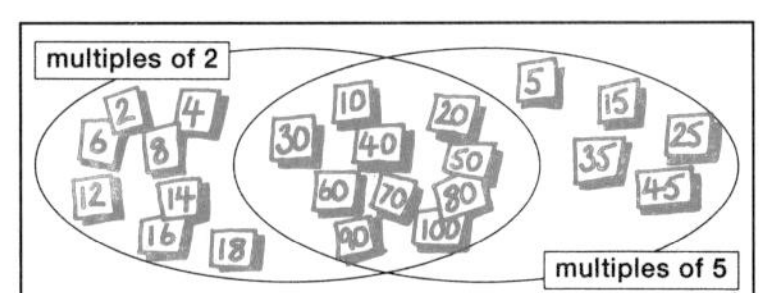

8

Answers in both the x2 and x5 tables = multiples of 10.

Answers in the x2 table but not in the x5 table = 2, 4, 6, 8, 12, 14, 16, 18.

Answers in the x5 table but not in the x2 table = 5, 15, 25, 35, 45.

Answers in the x2 table and not in the x5 table = 2, 4, 6, 8, 12, 14, 16, 18.

RESOURCE MASTER 89

Open: interpreting a 10 x 10 multiplication grid.
(1/3 a,c)

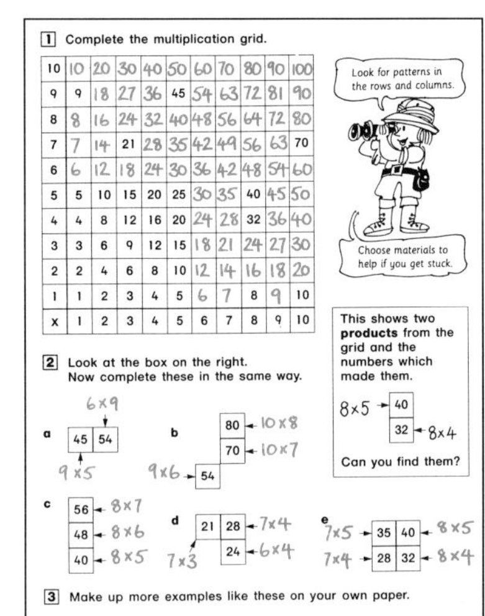

1 Complete the multiplication grid.

10	10	20	30	40	50	60	70	80	90	100
9	9	18	27	36	45	54	63	72	81	90
8	8	16	24	32	40	48	56	64	72	80
7	7	14	21	28	35	42	49	56	63	70
6	6	12	18	24	30	36	42	48	54	60
5	5	10	15	20	25	30	35	40	45	50
4	4	8	12	16	20	24	28	32	36	40
3	3	6	9	12	15	18	21	24	27	30
2	2	4	6	8	10	12	14	16	18	20
1	1	2	3	4	5	6	7	8	9	10
x	1	2	3	4	5	6	7	8	9	10

Look for patterns in the rows and columns.

Choose materials to help if you get stuck.

2 Look at the box on the right.
Now complete these in the same way.

This shows two **products** from the grid and the numbers which made them.

8×5 → 40
32 ← 8×4

Can you find them?

a 45 54; 6×9 → 54; 9×5 → 45

b 80 ← 10×8; 70 ← 10×7; 9×6 → 54

c 56 ← 8×7; 48 ← 8×6; 40 ← 8×5

d 21 28 ← 7×4; 24 ← 6×4; 7×3 → 21

e 7×5 → 35 40 ← 8×5; 7×4 → 28 32 ← 8×4

3 Make up more examples like these on your own paper.

RESOURCE MASTER 90

1

x2		x5		x10	
2 →	4	3 →	15	4 →	40
9 →	18	5 →	25	10 →	100
3 →	6	4 →	20	3 →	30
7 →	14	9 →	45	5 →	50
1 →	2	1 →	5	8 →	80
10 →	20	10 →	50	1 →	10
5 →	10	8 →	40	7 →	70
4 →	8	2 →	10	9 →	90
6 →	12	7 →	35	2 →	20
8 →	16	6 →	30	6 →	60

2

x6 0, 6, 12, 18, 24, 30, 36, 42, 48, 54, 60

x9 0, 9, 18, 27, 36, 45, 54, 63, 72, 81, 90

3

£30

4

90p

RESOURCE MASTER 91

1

a	14	**b**	15	**c**	18
d	12	**e**	50	**f**	30

2

a	16 10	**b**	90 72	**c**	27 35
d	43 8	**e**	0 30	**f**	13 9

3

a (2 + 3) x 2 = 10

b (10 – 6) x 5 = 20

c 5 x (8 + 2) = 50

d (10 x 5) – 1 = 49

e (8 + 2) x 9 = 90

f 5 x (2 + 4) = 30

RESOURCE MASTER 92

1 Find different ways of making the number shown in the stars. Use +, – and x every time.

2 Use ÷ if you want.

Some examples:

RESOURCE MASTER 96

Practical: constructing a net for a tetrahedron from given information.

RESOURCE MASTER 97

Practical: constructing a cube from a provided net and instructions.

RESOURCE MASTER 95

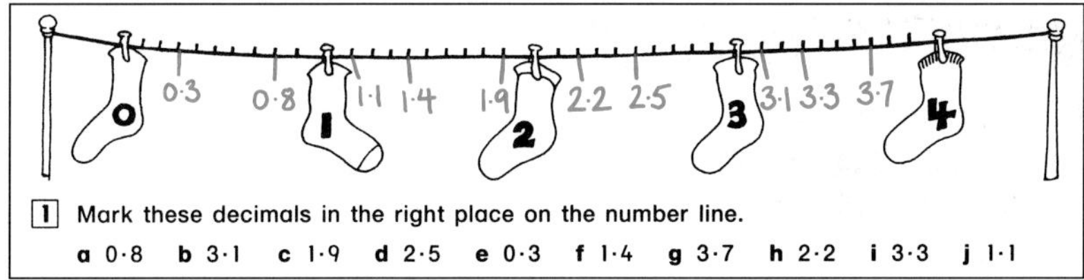

1 Mark these decimals in the right place on the number line.

a 0·8 **b** 3·1 **c** 1·9 **d** 2·5 **e** 0·3 **f** 1·4 **g** 3·7 **h** 2·2 **i** 3·3 **j** 1·1

2

a 0.8 < 1.4

b 3.3 > 0.3

c 2.5 > 1.9

d 2.2 < 3.7

e 3.1 > 0.8

f 1.1 < 1.4

3

a 0.9, 1.0, 1.1

b 3.0, 2.9, 2.8

c 1.5, 2.0, 2.5

d 1.4, 1.6, 1.8

4

a	2	**b**	2
c	4	**d**	0
e	1	**f**	1
g	3	**h**	3

RESOURCE MASTER 98

1

Shape	It is a prism.	It has 5 faces.	It has right-angled corners
cube	✔	✘	✔
cuboid	✔	✘	✔
triangular prism	✔	✔	✔
tetrahedron	✘	✘	✘
pyramid	✘	✔	✔
cylinder	✔	✘	✘
cone	✘	✘	✘
sphere	✘	✘	✘
hemisphere	✘	✘	✘

2

4 are prisms.

5 are not prisms.

2 have 5 faces.

7 do not have 5 faces

4 have right-angled corners.

5 do not have right-angled corners.

RESOURCE MASTER 99

Open: describing 3-D shapes using mathamatical terms. (1/3 b)

RESOURCE MASTER 101

Open: play the game.

RESOURCE MASTER 102

Open: using additional facts to solve problems. (1/3 a,c)

4

Open: using addition facts (totals to 20) to solve problems (1/3 a,c)

RESOURCE MASTER 103

1

a 6 **b** 10 **c** 6 **d** 9 **e** 8

f 7 **g** 5 **h** 9 **i** 11 **j** 8

2

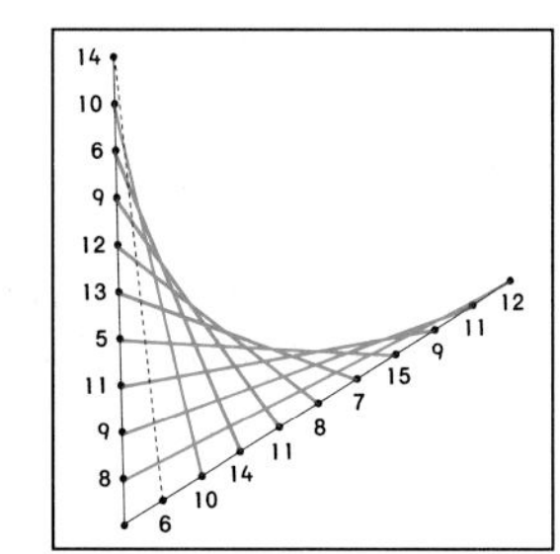

3

input (+ 8)	output
1	9
6	14
4	12
8	16
2	10
5	13
9	17
3	11
7	15

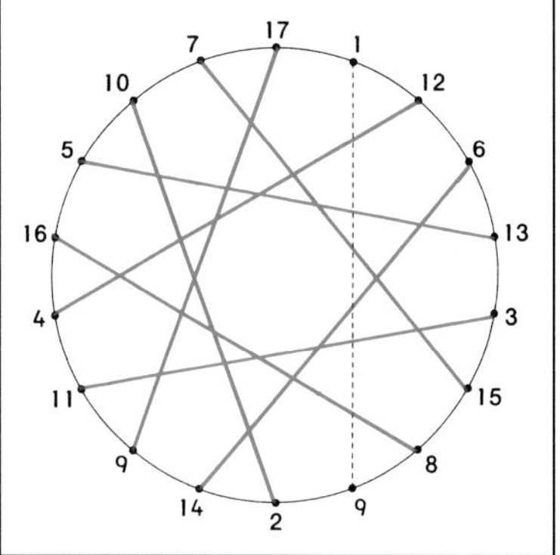

RESOURCE MASTER 105

1

a 130 **b** 150 **c** 120

d 60 **e** 90 **f** 80

2

a 140

c 10

b 50

d 90

3

Many possibilities.

(1/3 a,b,c)

RESOURCE MASTER 106

1

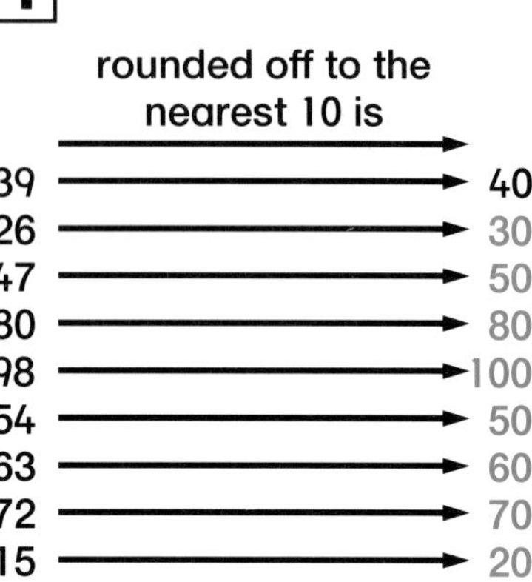

rounded off to the nearest 10 is

39 → 40
26 → 30
47 → 50
80 → 80
98 → 100
54 → 50
63 → 60
72 → 70
15 → 20

2

	approximate answer	actual answer
39 + 54	40 + 50 = 90	93
26 + 39	30 + 40 = 70	65
47 + 81	50 + 80 = 130	128
81 + 98	80 + 100 = 180	179
54 + 63	50 + 60 = 110	117
72 + 15	70 + 20 = 90	87
63 + 39	60 + 40 = 100	102
81 + 26	80 + 30 = 110	107
98 + 47	100 + 50 = 150	145

Check. Are your approximate answers sensible?

3

a 90 **b** 120 **c** 100

d 200 **e** 80 **f** 120

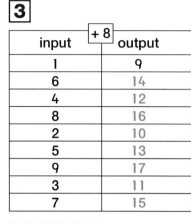

RESOURCE MASTER 107

1 – 2

Open: choose shapes, predict then check the conclusions.

3

Open: predictions will vary. The correct answers are listed below:

hexagon	6
oblong	2
semi-cricle	1
quarter-circle	1
rhombus	2
pentagon	5
square	4

RESOURCE MASTER 108

Practical: play the game.

Challenge

10 x 3, 6 x 5, 5 x 6

RESOURCE MASTER 109

Practical: play the game.

RESOURCE MASTER 110

1

Actual number
9
7
8
11
8
13
90
12
14

2

Actual number	Length left over
5	3 cm
9	4 cm
10	1 cm
9	3 cm
8	4 cm
10	8 cm

RESOURCE MASTER 111

1 – 3

40 ÷ 5	(< 10) = 10 > 10	8
72 ÷ 6	< 10 = 10 (> 10)	12
90 ÷ 10	(< 10) = 10 > 10	9
56 ÷ 8	(< 10) = 10 > 10	7
50 ÷ 5	< 10 (= 10) > 10	10
63 ÷ 9	(< 10) = 10 > 10	7
76 ÷ 4	< 10 = 10 (> 10)	14
70 ÷ 7	< 10 (= 10) > 10	10
96 ÷ 8	< 10 = 10 (> 10)	12
42 ÷ 7	(< 10) = 10 > 10	6

4

Open: halving numbers between 50 and 100.

5

When I divide an **even** number by 2, the answer is a whole number.

When I divide an **odd** number by 2, the answer is not a whole number; it ends in ·5.

RESOURCE MASTER 112

1

÷ 2	÷ 5	÷ 10
10 → 5	10 → 2	10 → 1
6 → 3	15 → 3	90 → 9
20 → 10	35 → 7	80 → 8
8 → 4	30 → 6	30 → 3
2 → 1	5 → 1	70 → 7
14 → 7	40 → 8	20 → 2
18 → 9	25 → 5	60 → 6
12 → 6	50 → 10	50 → 5
16 → 8	45 → 9	40 → 4
4 → 2	20 → 4	100 → 10

2

a 14 **b** 9 remainder 2

c 9 p **d** 9 cards each. 3 cards left over.

RESOURCE MASTER 113

Practical: play the game.

RESOURCE MASTER 114

Practical: play the game.

RESOURCE MASTER 115

1

a 110
b 90
c 60
d 110
e 160
f 150

2

a 80
b 100
c 40
d 40

3

Open: mental subtraction of numbers upto 200. (1/3 a,b)

RESOURCE MASTER 116

1

rounded off to the nearest 10 is →

29	→	30
64	→	60
86	→	90
152	→	150
78	→	80
133	→	130
175	→	180
101	→	100
197	→	200

2

	approximate answer	actual answer
64 – 29	60 – 30 = 30	35
133 – 78	130 – 80 = 50	55
152 – 64	150 – 60 = 90	88
101 – 86	100 – 90 = 10	15
86 – 29	90 – 30 = 60	57
175 – 101	180 – 100 = 80	74
78 – 64	80 – 60 = 20	14
175 – 78	180 – 80 = 100	97
197 – 101	200 – 100 = 100	96

3

a 100 **b** 40 **c** 30

d 20 **e** 50 **f** 70

RESOURCE MASTER 117

Open: solving problems using 2-D shapes. (1/3 a,c)

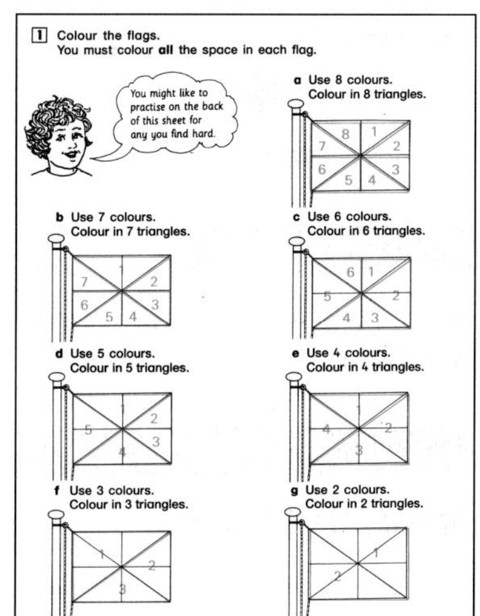

RESOURCE MASTER 118

Open: drawing quadrilaterals, pentagons, hexagons; identifying angles. (1/3 a,b,c)

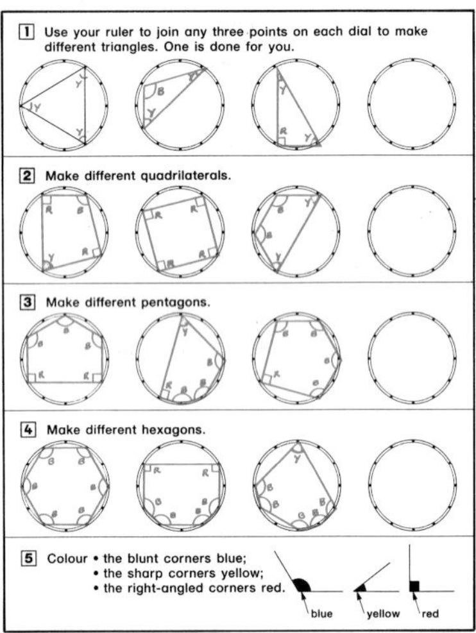

1 Use your ruler to join any three points on each dial to make different triangles. One is done for you.
2 Make different quadrilaterals.
3 Make different pentagons.
4 Make different hexagons.
5 Colour • the blunt corners blue; • the sharp corners yellow; • the right-angled corners red.
blue
yellow
red

RESOURCE MASTER 119

Open: measuring capacities to the nearest 10 ml.

RESOURCE MASTER 120

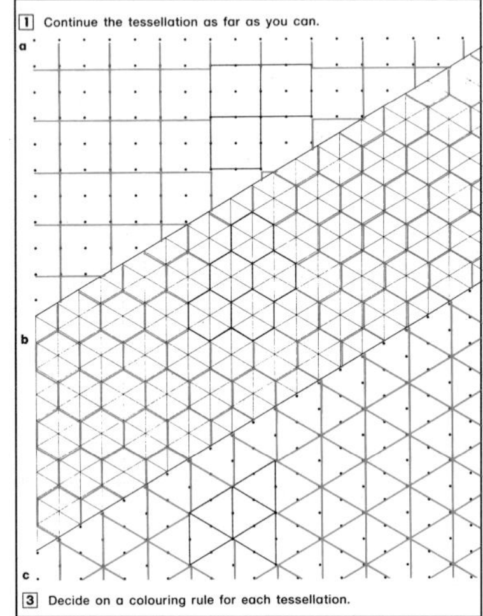

1 Continue the tessellation as far as you can.
a
b
c
3 Decide on a colouring rule for each tessellation.

RESOURCE MASTER 121

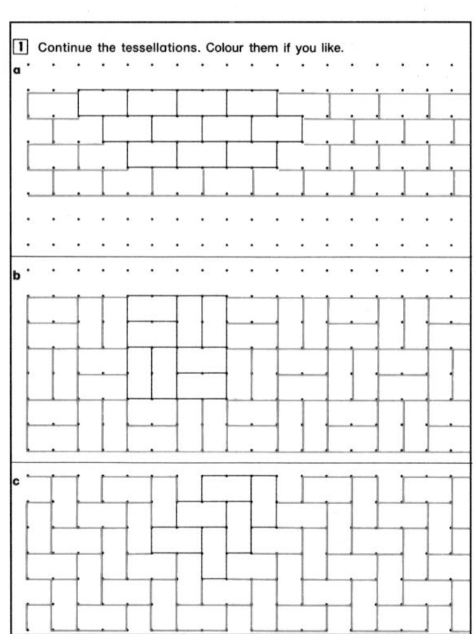

1 Continue the tessellations. Colour them if you like.
a
b
c

RESOURCE MASTER 122

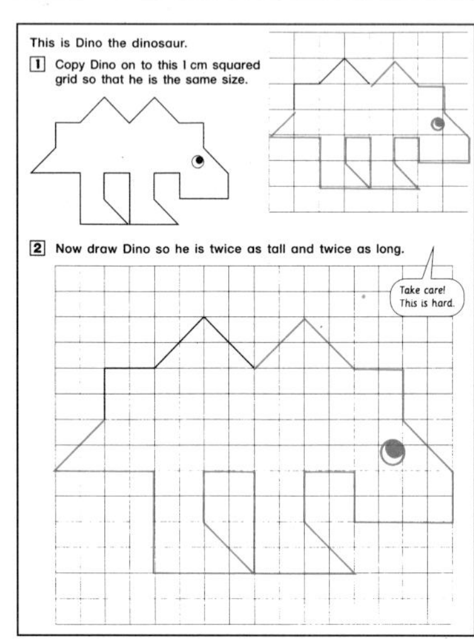

This is Dino the dinosaur.
1 Copy Dino on to this 1 cm squared grid so that he is the same size.
2 Now draw Dino so he is twice as tall and twice as long.
Take care! This is hard.

RESOURCE MASTER 123

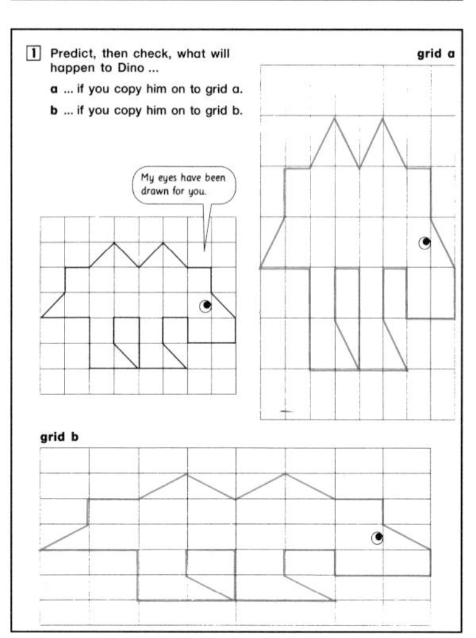

a ... if you copy him on to grid a.
b ... if you copy him on to grid b.

My eyes have been drawn for you.

RESOURCE MASTER 125

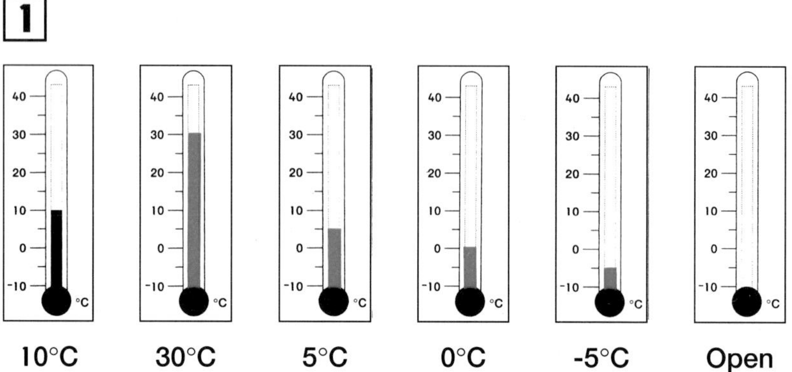

RESOURCE MASTER 127

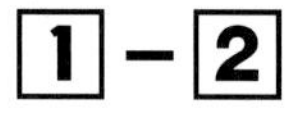

From	To	Up	Down
Car park	Toys	6	
Toys	Books		1
Books and Records	Children's clothes	2	
Children's clothes	Kitchen goods		4
Kitchen goods	Electrical goods		1
Electrical goods	Gardening		1
Gardening	Coffee shop	9	
Coffee shop	Car park		10

3

From	To	Up	Down
car park	Kitchen goods	3	
Kitchen goods	Gardening		2
Gardening	Electrical goods	1	
Electrical goods	Books	3	
Books	Toys	1	
Toys	Children's clothes	1	
Children's clothes	Coffee shop	3	
Coffee shop	Car park		10

RESOURCE MASTER 128

1

3 x	x 3
3 x 0 = 0	0 x 3 = 0
3 x 1 = 3	1 x 3 = 3
3 x 2 = 6	2 x 3 = 6
3 x 3 = 9	3 x 3 = 9
3 x 4 = 12	4 x 3 = 12
3 x 5 = 15	5 x 3 = 15
3 x 6 = 18	6 x 3 = 18
3 x 7 = 21	7 x 3 = 21
3 x 8 = 24	8 x 3 = 24
3 x 9 = 27	9 x 3 = 27
3 x 10 = 30	10 x 3 = 30

2

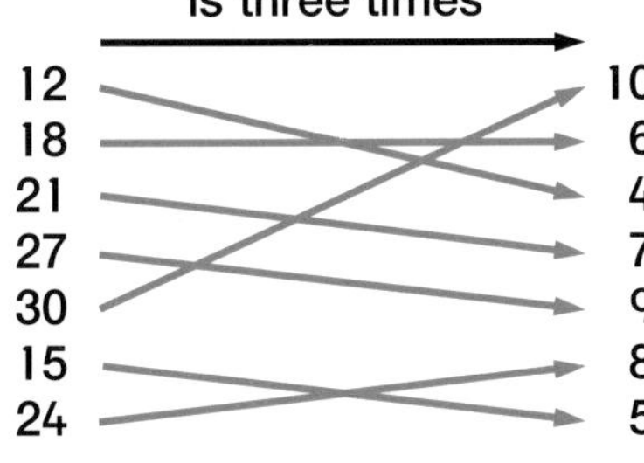

3

a 3 **b** 9 **c** 7

d 8 **e** 6 **f** 9

4

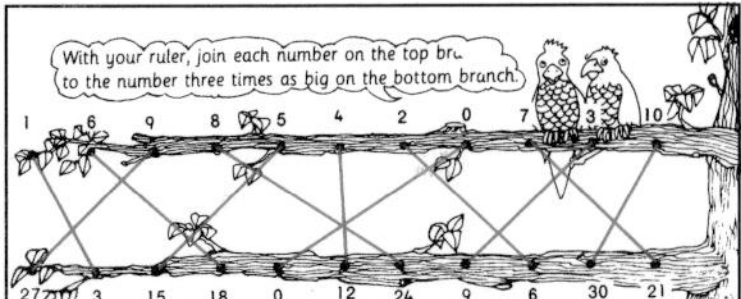

to the number three times as big on the bottom branch.

RESOURCE MASTER 129

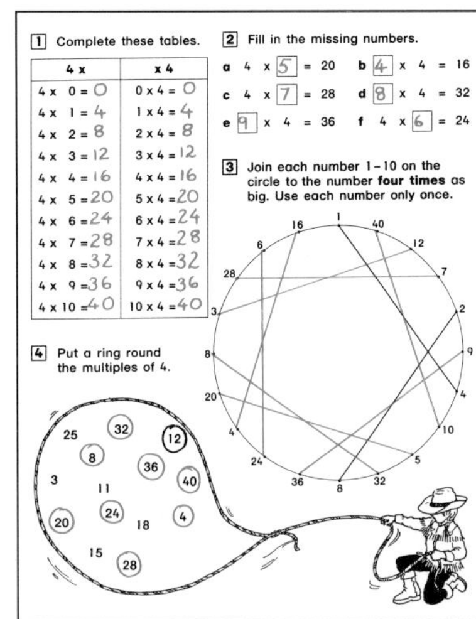

1 Complete these tables.

4 x	x 4
4 x 0 = 0	0 x 4 = 0
4 x 1 = 4	1 x 4 = 4
4 x 2 = 8	2 x 4 = 8
4 x 3 = 12	3 x 4 = 12
4 x 4 = 16	4 x 4 = 16
4 x 5 = 20	5 x 4 = 20
4 x 6 = 24	6 x 4 = 24
4 x 7 = 28	7 x 4 = 28
4 x 8 = 32	8 x 4 = 32
4 x 9 = 36	9 x 4 = 36
4 x 10 = 40	10 x 4 = 40

2 Fill in the missing numbers.

a 4 x 5 = 20 **b** 4 x 4 = 16

c 4 x 7 = 28 **d** 8 x 4 = 32

e 9 x 4 = 36 **f** 4 x 6 = 24

3 Join each number 1 – 10 on the circle to the number **four times** as big. Use each number only once.

4 Put a ring round the multiples of 4.

RESOURCE MASTER 130

21 divided by 3 is 7
7 doubled is 14
14 divided by 7 is 2
2 multiplied by 10 is 20
20 divided by 4 is 5
4 multiplied by 10 is 40
40 divided by 5 is 8
8 multiplied by 3 is 24
24 divided by 4 is 6
6 trebled is 18
18 halved is 9
9 multiplied by 4 is 36
36 divided by 4 is 9
9 divided by 3 is 3
3 multiplied by 10 is 30
30 divided by 5 is 6
6 multiplied by 4 is 24
24 divided by 3 is 8
8 multiplied by 4 is 32
32 divided by 4 is 8
8 multiplied by 5 is 40
40 divided by 4 is 10
10 multiplied by 7 is 70
70 divided by 10 is 7
7 multiplied by 3 is 21

RESOURCE MASTER 131

1

Many possibilities. Some examples are listed:

2 x4 = 8	2 x 2 = 4
20 x 4 = 80	20 x 2 = 40
5 x 7 = 35	7 x 8 = 56
50 x 7 = 350	70 x 8 = 560
4 x 3 = 12	5 x 4 = 20
40 x 3 = 120	50 x 4 = 200

2

a 100 **b** 120 **c** 240 160

RESOURCE MASTER 133

1

a 5E ➔ 2S ➔ 3W ➔ 2S ➔ 5E
4N ➔ 5E ➔ 2S ➔ 3W ➔ 2S
5E ➔ 4N ➔ 5E ➔ 2S ➔ 3W
2S ➔ 5E

b 5W ➔ 2N ➔ 3E ➔ 2N ➔ 5W
4S ➔ 5W ➔ 2N ➔ 3E ➔ 2N
5W ➔ 4S ➔ 5W ➔ 2N ➔ 3E
2N ➔ 5W

2

7 Go through front door

6 Walk 7 strides

5 Go down 15 stairs

4 Turn right

3 Walk 5 strides

2 Turn left

1 Leave bedroom

RESOURCE MASTER 134

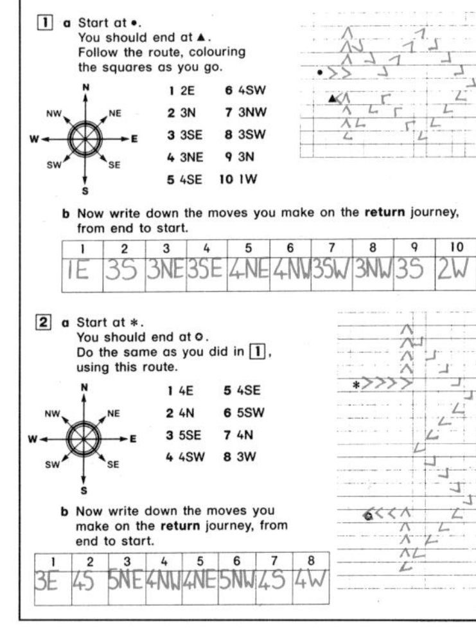

1 **a** Start at •.
You should end at ▲.
Follow the route, colouring the squares as you go.

1 2E 6 4SW
2 3N 7 3NW
3 3SE 8 3SW
4 3NE 9 3N
5 4SE 10 1W

b Now write down the moves you make on the **return** journey, from end to start.

1	2	3	4	5	6	7	8	9	10
1E	3S	3NE	3SE	4NE	4NW	3SW	3NW	3S	2W

2 **a** Start at *.
You should end at ○.
Do the same as you did in **1**, using this route.

1 4E 5 4SE
2 4N 6 5SW
3 5SE 7 4N
4 4SW 8 3W

b Now write down the moves you make on the **return** journey, from end to start.

1	2	3	4	5	6	7	8
3E	4S	5NE	4NW	4NE	5NW	4S	4W

RESOURCE MASTER 135

1

	rounded off to the nearest 100 is
127	100
342	300
205	200
397	400
493	500
520	500
717	700
684	700
278	300

2

	approximate answer	actual answer
127 + 684	100 + 700 = 800	811
342 + 397	300 + 400 = 700	739
205 + 493	200 + 500 = 700	698
520 + 397	500 + 400 = 900	917
684 + 205	700 + 200 = 900	889
717 + 278	700 + 300 = 1000	995
278 + 342	300 + 300 = 600	620
397 + 342	400 + 300 = 700	739
493 + 520	500 + 500 = 1000	1013

3

a 400 **b** 1000

c 1000 **d** 900

e 800 **f** 1000

g 500 **h** 700

RESOURCE MASTER 136

1

rounded off to the nearest 100 is

129	→	100
322	→	300
580	→	600
998	→	1000
706	→	700
386	→	400
479	→	500
841	→	800
267	→	300

2

	approximate answer	actual answer
386 – 267	400 - 300 = 100	119
580 – 267	600 - 300 = 300	313
706 – 322	700 - 300 = 400	384
841 – 129	800 - 100 = 700	712
479 – 386	500 - 400 = 100	93
998 – 479	1000 - 500 = 500	519
841 – 322	800 - 300 = 500	519
998 – 386	1000 - 400 = 600	612
841 – 706	800 - 700 = 100	135

3

a 400 **b** 200

c 200 **d** 400

e 100 **f** 200

g 700 **h** 400

RESOURCE MASTER 137

1

a 223 **b** 319 **c** 383

d 267 **e** 509 **f** 525

g 854 **h** 677 **i** 386

2

a 666 – 125 = 541

b 319 – 125 = 194

c 817 – 125 = 692

d 508 – 125 = 383

e 966 – 125 = 841

f 731 – 125 = 606

3

Open: using materials to solve subtraction problems using numbers to 999.

For example:

518 – 242 = 176

324 – 158 = 166

845 – 213 = 632

(1/3 a,b,c)

RESOURCE MASTER 138

Open: solving addition and subtraction problems using numbers to 999. (1/3 a,b)

1
512

2
512

3
419

4
£847, £153

Challenge

Write own stories.

RESOURCE MASTER 139

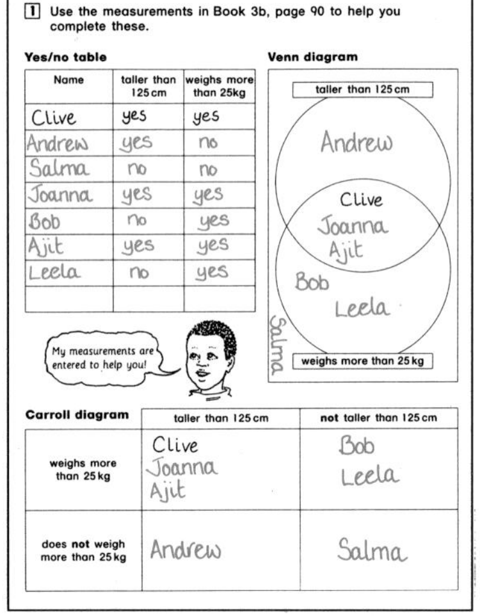

1 Use the measurements in Book 3b, page 90 to help you complete these.

Yes/no table

Name	taller than 125 cm	weighs more than 25 kg
Clive	yes	yes
Andrew	yes	no
Salma	no	no
Joanna	yes	yes
Bob	no	yes
Ajit	yes	yes
Leela	no	yes

Venn diagram

taller than 125 cm: Andrew

both: Clive, Joanna, Ajit

weighs more than 25 kg: Bob, Leela

outside: Salma

Carroll diagram

	taller than 125 cm	not taller than 125 cm
weighs more than 25 kg	Clive, Joanna, Ajit	Bob, Leela
does not weigh more than 25 kg	Andrew	Salma

RESOURCE MASTER 142

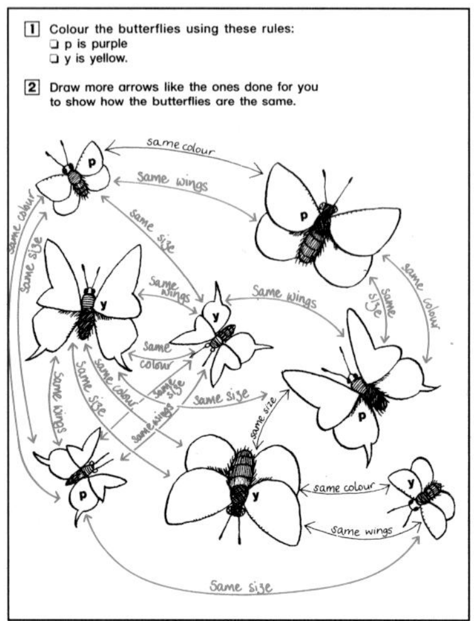

1 Colour the butterflies using these rules:
❑ p is purple
❑ y is yellow.

2 Draw more arrows like the ones done for you to show how the butterflies are the same.